The
Somersetshire
Coal Canal
Rediscovered

A Walker's Guide

Niall Allsop

Millstream Books

for Kieron, Jamie and Kristin

First published 1988; second edition 1993

Millstream Books
7 Orange Grove
Bath BA1 1LP

This book is set in Helvetica
This edition produced at Cornerhouse, Manchester
Printed in Great Britain by The Matthews Wright Press, Chard, Somerset

© Niall Allsop 1988 and 1993

ISBN 0948975350

Cover illustrations:
front, lock 15 of the Combe Hay flight and the decaying gates of lock 9
rear, Rev John Skinner's watercolour of the canal in use at Durcott,
painted c1820s, from the Rev R E S Bennett Collection

Contents

Acknowledgements

For his meticulous research on behalf of the Avon Industrial Buildings Trust, his generosity in sharing this, his painstaking scrutiny of the manuscript and his imaginative reconstruction of the Caisson Lock, I am indebted to Mike Chapman.

For helping create a constructive and happy working relationship with AIBT, above and beyond the call of duty, my thanks to Rosie Northcote and Mary Stacey.

For their previously published researches, the following authors have been invaluable sources:

Kenneth Clew: *The Somersetshire Coal Canal and Railways*,
    David & Charles (1970)
Peter Collier: *Colliers' Way*, Ex Libris Press (1986)
Chris Handley: *The Railways & Tramways of Radstock*, Somerset and Dorset
    Railway Museum Trust (1980)
Hugh Torrens: 'The Somersetshire Coal Canal Caisson Lock' *BIAS*, Vol 8 (1975)
Chris Howell: *Round here, in them days*, privately published (1980)
P J G Ransom: *The Archaeology of the Transport Revolution 1750-1850*,
    World's Work (1984)

For putting pen to paper in the hope that others might find something of value in their experiences and recollections we are all indebted to:

Rev John Skinner, Rector of Camerton - *Journal of a Somerset Rector 1803-1834*, edited by Howard and Peter Coombes, Kingsmead Press (1971).
Sydney Bourne – letter to *Country Life*, May 11th 1951.
S Lloyd Harvey – as quoted in the *Somerset Guardian*, August 8th 1958.
George Tucker – as quoted in the *Somerset Guardian*, April 26th 1968.

For permission to use their photographs and/or other prints, special thanks to AIBT, Bath Reference Library, Len Bampfylde, Kennet & Avon Canal Trust, Edward Smith, Gordon Tucker and Tim Wheeldon. For their research facilities and assistance I am most grateful to the staff of Bath Reference Library and Bath Evening Chronicle. For photograph processing many thanks to Steve Chandler. For transport in the absence of buses I couldn't have done without Maggie Dunn, Jan and Phil Keen and Harry Harrison. To Maggie Dunn, Jan and Phil Keen, Rosie Northcote ... a simple 'thanks' for your friendship throughout. To Kay Bowen, Linda Dunn, Alan Ward and Tim Graham special thanks for sharing the walking in researching this edition; thanks too to Stephanie Laidler for typing the amendments.

Introduction

In 1983 the April edition of the national waterways magazine, *Canal & Riverboat*, carried an article (see Appendix B) on the restoration to a navigable standard of the Somersetshire Coal Canal. A two-year blitz on the derelict canal had, seemingly, paid dividends and, with the assistance of the ingenious Single Inclined Lock, there was to be no stopping the festivities on Good Friday . . . April 1st!

As the instigator of these unlikely events I took not a little pleasure in conning some members of the waterways fraternity who should have known better but was more contrite upon discovering that some local enthusiasts had, even before the fateful day, donned their walking gear, stocked up with Yorkie bars and headed SCC-wards. I cannot be certain whether or not it was the intricacies of the Single Inclined Lock, the prospect of seeing boats on the move or the imaginary canalside Nudist Camp that took their fancy; in concluding that it was probably not the latter I am, I suppose, justifying the writing of this book.

But there is more to it than that. Unknown to me at the time there were others interested in the canal and in particular the state of the Combe Hay Locks, some of which were clearly in danger of disappearing altogether. These 'others' were given substance in 1984 as the Avon Industrial Buildings Trust (AIBT) under whose auspices every inch of the canal's Dunkerton and Radstock lines has now been meticulously surveyed and recorded.

The story of the Somersetshire Coal Canal is as intriguing as it is unique – no more so than in the mystery surrounding the location of the inspiration for my Single Inclined Lock, Robert Weldon's equally bizarre, but certainly more feasible, Caisson Lock. The SCC's junction with the Kennet & Avon Canal at Dundas is also veiled in uncertainty but less mysterious is the canal's natural and industrial environment which, though it leaves much to the imagination, is no mere ditch-side stroll.

I therefore offer this journey through the Somersetshire Coal Canal's past and present not only in recognition of the work accomplished by AIBT but also as a belated apology to those who believed in '83 . . . in the hope that they, and others, will seek out and appreciate what remains of the canal and in so doing absorb a little of its inimitable spirit.

Since the first edition of this book, the Somersetshire Coal Canal Society has been formed to foster interest in the canal. Details can be obtained from Derrick Hunt, Greystones, 7 Carlingcott, Peasedown St John, Bath BA2 8AR; tel: (0761) 434618 or from Tim Wheeldon, The Somersetshire Coal Canal Co, Brass Knocker Bottom, Monkton Combe, Bath BA2 7JD; tel: (0225) 722292. A permanent Museum/ Interpretation Centre is planned at Brass Knocker Bottom where it is hoped that all SCC documents, relics, etc, may be assembled under one roof. At present most items of SCC interest are in the custody of the Bath Industrial Heritage Centre or the Radstock, Midsomer Norton & District Museum Society.

The Somersetshire Coal Canal: Dawn to Dusk

> . . . between the Hours of Eight o'Clock, on Thursday Night, and Four o'Clock on Friday morning, the 15th and 16th of November, 1738, the Lock at Solford [*sic*] was almost destroyed by Persons unknown; who left two threatening Papers, which declared in Substance, That an Attempt was made only by Three Hundred Men, as the beginning of much greater Mischief that was intended against the navigation, by as many Thousand, unless an immediate Stop was put to the sending of any more Coals by Water.

Thus did John Wood in his *An Essay towards a Description of Bath* describe the result of anger aroused locally by the importation of Shropshire coal via the Avon Navigation, opened between Bristol and Bath in 1727. The 'Persons unknown' are generally believed to have been Somerset colliers who, not surprisingly, saw such imports in general and the Avon Navigation in particular as a threat to their own livelihoods. Despite the incentive of a reward for information, the culprits were never caught; nor did the thousands on stand-by ever materialise. In the North Somerset coalfields the hardship and drudgery of life went on; in the valley of the Avon the navigation, despite its unpredictable nature, continued to prosper; the fires of Bath burnt brighter.

In the mid 18th century the extraction of coal in North Somerset was still in its infancy, not only in terms of the technology but also in its organisation. All that was to change when, in 1763, James Lansdown discovered a deep seam at Radstock where it had hitherto been deemed too difficult to mine. The pit became known as Upper Radstock and soon further shafts were sunk in and around Radstock, Timsbury, Paulton and Camerton. The Somerset coalfield was born and with it a need to have an efficient and cheap means of exporting such a sought-after natural resource.

Elsewhere too there was change in the air. It was but a short mental leap from exploiting navigable rivers to building man-made watery arteries and so the twilight of the century was given fresh impetus by the canal-building fervour that crept south from Britain's industrial heartland. By 1792 the prospect of cheaper Welsh coal sweeping through the Avon valley in the wake of the cutting of the Monmouthshire Canal caused the Somerset colliery owners to embrace 'the propriety of making a navigable canal from the several collieries to this city [Bath]'.

By 1793 the pace had quickened. A committee was formed empowered to 'employ and direct one or more able engineer or engineers to survey, plan and make estimates of the expence of completing such lines of canal and branches for the accommodation of the Northern collieries, as they may conceive most practicable and advantageous. And at the same time, that such engineer or engineers be directed to survey the expence of making a branch from the proposed canal to Radstock.' The chosen engineer was John Rennie who at the time was much involved locally in the Western Canal (later the Kennet & Avon) project; it was his report later that year that was to be the basis for the main line route from the Kennet & Avon at

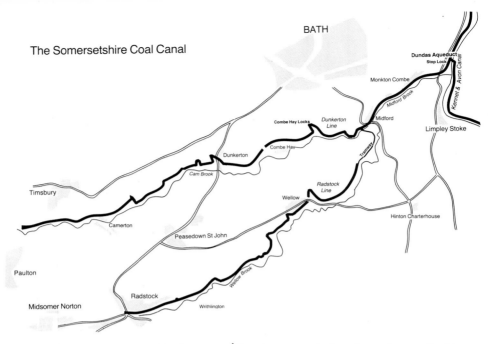

The Somersetshire Coal Canal

BATH

Dundas Aqueduct
Stop Lock

Kennet & Avon Canal

Monkton Combe

Midford Brook

Combe Hay Locks — Dunkerton Line — Midford

Limpley Stoke

Dunkerton

Combe Hay

Radstock Line

Cam Brook

Wellow

Tunnel

Timsbury

Hinton Charterhouse

Camerton

Peasedown St John

Wellow Brook

Paulton

Radstock

Midsomer Norton

Writhlington

Dundas to Paulton Basin near Timsbury and the branch south to Radstock.

A more direct route to Bath was discounted on the basis that Dundas would not only give easy and lock-free access to Bath via the Kennet & Avon but also east into Wiltshire. This strategy was to pay dividends, the more so with the cutting of the Wilts & Berks Canal which, via Semington on the Kennet & Avon, opened up markets for Somerset's coal in North Wiltshire and Oxfordshire. Coincidentally, on April 17th 1794, both the Kennet & Avon Canal Act and the Somersetshire Coal Canal Act received the Royal Assent, their future inter-dependency foreseen in the preamble to the latter:

> An Act for making and maintaining a Navigable Canal, with certain Rail Ways, and Stone Roads, from several Collieries, in the County of *Somerset*, to communicate with the intended *Kennet* and *Avon* Canal, in the Parish of *Bradford*, in the County of *Wilts*.

Two years later a second Act embodied several alterations to the original route, deviations which took the proposed canal to a higher level to obviate the need for a long tunnel at Combe Hay. Although several other respected canal engineers – notably William Jessop and Robert Whitworth – had assisted Rennie with new surveys, it was William Bennet and Rennie's young understudy, William Smith, who were destined to become the figures most associated with the canal and its construction. In 1794 Smith had accompanied two of the Canal Company's committee on an epic 900-mile tour of the country's embryonic waterway network to establish '. . . the most beneficial mode of carrying this canal and the railroads into execution . . .'. It is not clear whether or not the trio visited the Coalbrookdale area of Shropshire where Robert Weldon was demonstrating his 'Patent Hydrostatick or Caisson-lock'; three members of the Kennet & Avon's committee did visit the site and it was their small model of the caisson that persuaded the SCC committee to experiment with Weldon's invention on *their* canal at Combe Hay.

The caisson lock is dealt with in greater detail in Walk 2 and Appendix A – suffice to record here the briefest of details. While work progressed east and west of Combe Hay and on the Radstock branch, the stumbling block (other than money) to any possibility of through navigation was the deficiencies, real and imagined, of the caisson lock. Weldon's optimism was thwarted by a series of technical hitches, given short-lived substance by a visit from the Prince of Wales and finally broken by bulging brickwork and the Committee's decision in 1800 to discontinue the experiment in favour of an inclined plane. No doubt their judgment was influenced by the nature of the topographical problem at Combe Hay which would have necessitated three or even four such locks.

The obvious, albeit commonplace and time-consuming, answer to the problem of 'making the communication between the upper and lower Level' at Combe Hay was, of course, a flight of locks. But this was a time of innovative technology, of fertile minds determined to make possible the impossible. Among the contenders for stepping into Weldon's shoes (if not his despair) were Messrs Norton and Whitmore with their geometrical lock, James Fussell with his balance lock and Ralph Dodd and Benjamin Outram with alternative versions of the inclined plane. In June 1800, after much indecision and not a little acrimony between the proponents of the various schemes, the SCC committee decided to 'regulate the descent of the waggons carrying boxes of a ton of coals each on an inclined plane, which are linked to an endless chain passing round a cylindrical wheel at the upper and one of the same diameter at the lower end'. The deep cutting at the bottom of the plane was to be 'saved by 3 locks'. Although Outram is not mentioned by name his status elsewhere as a canal engineer would suggest that it was his rather than Dodd's version that won the day.

The three locks were a hint of the inevitable. Back in April 1800 John Sutcliffe (engineer on the canal between 1794 and 1795) had reported that 'when every circumstance and conveniency are impartially examined, that will attend making it [joining the upper and lower levels] by common Locks, it will far exceed any other Plan that can be devised, and will ultimately be found most advantageous to the Company, and beneficial to the Public, notwithstanding the first expence may far exceed that . . . of inclined Planes'. The inevitable was, as Sutcliffe astutely foresaw, a flight of locks, for although in November 1801 the *Gloucester Journal* announced that the canal was 'now so complete as to convey barges from the Timsbury and other pits, to the junction of the Kennet & Avon Canal', the inclined plane effectively highlighted its *incompleteness* and was thus literally a stop-gap measure until such time as the financial will was there to construct locks.

It is almost impossible to separate the fortunes of the western end of the Kennet & Avon from those of the SCC. From May 1801 the Foxhangers (Devizes) to Bath section of the former was in water and with it the incentive to assure the efficient carriage of coal down to Bath. The fact that the Kennet & Avon Canal Company saw the inclined plane as 'extremely inconvenient and difficult to pass' was but confirmation to the SCC committee that it should go, and with it plans for a second plane on the

Radstock arm. Thus, in 1802, a third Somersetshire Coal Canal Act received the Royal Assent empowering the committee to raise sufficient money to replace the inclined plane with locks. In this the SCC was assisted by the proprietors of the Kennet & Avon and the Wilts & Berks Canals by the formation of a 'Lock Fund'.

While the problems around Combe Hay may have caught the public imagination, work did progress elsewhere on the main Dundas-Paulton line, though less so south towards Radstock. Advertisements for tenders first appeared in the local press in May 1795:

> The committee will be ready on the 2nd June to receive proposals from any person willing to contract for cutting, embanking, puddling, and compleating that part of the canal from Paulton engine to or near a place called Hopyard, in the parish of Camerton, being in length about two miles; and also from Radstock Bridge to Peglinch, in the parish of Wellow, being about two miles; for building the several road and occupation bridges, and also for framing and laying out the proposed railroads, from the different collieries to the canal . . .

During the next few months tenders for similar stretches of canal – normally around two miles in length – were sought but it was not until late 1798 that the first section was in water when, on October 1st five coal-laden boats left Camerton colliery for Dunkerton from where two loads were taken to Bath 'on a good turnpike road'.

By the following May the navigable section had been extended west to Radford and to the canal's terminus at Paulton Basin in November; at the same time the cut between Radstock and Wellow was almost complete. And so it remained for over two years until, in November 1801, the Dunkerton arm from Dundas to Paulton was complete, albeit with the minor hiccup of the inclined plane at Combe Hay. The problems here cost

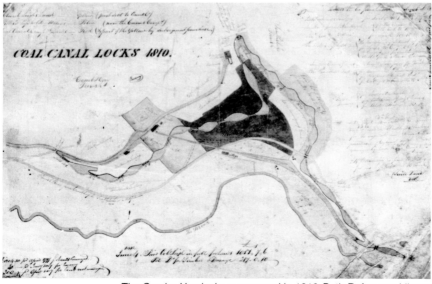

The Combe Hay locks as mapped in 1810. Bath Reference Library

money and the additional cost of locks meant that work on the Radstock arm all but ceased . . . despite the optimism implicit in the advertisement of June 1802 for

> any person or persons desirous of undertaking the Erection of an Aqueduct over the brook near Mitford and forming an embankment and part of the Canal from the intended Lower Lock on the Radstock line of canal to the proposed junction with the present canal near Mitford aforesaid . . .

But it was the provision of locks at Combe Hay that was the Canal Company's priority though their intention to '. . . receive proposals from and agree with any person or persons desirous of undertaking the Masonry of Nineteen Locks intended to be erected on the Radstock line and Seventeen Locks on the Dunkerton line . . .' was, at the time, genuine enough. Thus when, in April 1805, the *Gloucester Journal* reported that the proprietors had '. . . opened their locks (22 in number) at Combhay, which produces water communication between the coalpits, the Kennet & Avon and the Wilts & Berks Canals . . .' only one chamber on the Radstock arm had been constructed. At the same time a hint of what was to come was all but spelt out by the 'temporary' substitution of a mile-long tramroad between Twinhoe and Midford for the remaining 18 locks.

When, after 1810, both the K&A and the Wilts & Berks Canals were opened throughout and ripe for the conveyance of Somerset's coal, it was the Dunkerton line and its connecting collieries that profited from such new and far-flung markets. In contrast the Radstock arm was scarcely benefiting from the problems of transhipment at Twinhoe and Midford though these alone would seem insufficient explanation for its rapid drift into disuse. The local folk-memory that links its decline with lack of water has a familiar ring to it; the purported opposition by the owners of riparian rights by the Wellow Brook to its diversion as a feeder for the canal may thus have been an important, even crucial, factor. Whatever the reasons, there can be no doubt that by 1814 the concept of a canal link between the

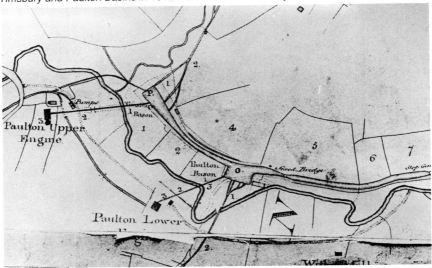

collieries in the Radstock area and the Dunkerton Line had been abandoned in favour of a 'New Rail Road' that not only incorporated the existing road between Twinhoe and Midford but also the tramroads between Radstock Basin and collieries further west at Clandown and Welton. This 'certain and regular communication' was 'cheerfully' opened in July 1815, its single track sited atop a towpath that now assumed authority over its erstwhile master – a canal-bed, redundant and waterless . . . a raw scar across the landscape that time would slowly heal . . . and ultimately forget.

Even allowing for its unusual, even bizarre, genesis, the fortunes of the SCC following the 'completion' of its two branches are not dissimilar to those that befell canals elsewhere in Britain. Initially both canal and tramway prospered as each served the trade in goods and people with almost unfettered enthusiasm . . . enthusiasm forgetful of the canal's early engineering successes and failures and thus blind to the inevitability of further reconnaisance into the technological minefield.

The Railway Age followed hot on the heels of the Canal Age, its reality but a short engineering leap from the SCC's own tramroad. The K&A and, to a lesser extent, the Wilts & Berks were the first to suffer. By 1841 the former had to contend with a rail link between Bristol and London and soon initiated an intense programme of futile competition which, in a little over a decade, ended ignominiously with the sale of the canal to its arch-rival, the Great Western Railway. To record that the SCC was less effected by the GWR is only to acknowledge a postponement of the inevitable; the K&A's plight was more immediate and the SCC was drawn into the battle (through, for example, being persuaded to reduce tolls) almost as a subordinate, albeit an important one. Initially the SCC's battles were more often with the K&ACC itself with whom it frequently refused to co-operate. For the latter the two canals were but extensions of each other; to the SCC, unthreatened by a railway plying the same route, the K&A's problems were not only less pressing but also fundamentally different.

As its name suggests, the SCC's trade was firmly established on the needs of one particular activity – the mining and transport of coal. The coming of the railways had thus an unusual and even contradictory dual effect on the canal; on the one hand the railways were an obvious rival for the carrying of goods and people; on the other hand, as the Somerset colliery owners were not slow to realize, the new technology itself created a market for their product. The Timsbury Coal Co, for example, rented a wharf at Bristol anticipating that it might cash in on fuelling the new steamships. Their enterprise was unsuccessful and the venture discontinued in 1860.

Coal mining itself was no less prone to new developments than the technological advances being made in the field of transport and, though the Somerset collieries were in no way at the forefront of such changes, output was on the increase. The opening of the GWR branch line between Frome and Radstock in 1854 was thus an obvious artery to be tapped by the coal companies and one which three years later they themselves sought to extend to Timsbury at their own expense. This scheme failed as did several others over the next decade but the Radstock-Frome line, with its branch to Ludlow's Colliery, soon began to pick up trade from the SCC though initially not as much as might have been expected.

Two schemes, however, did not fail. Though started in 1863, it was not until 1873 that the Bristol & North Somerset Railway, linking Radstock with Bristol, opened to traffic. But of more import was the planned extension of the Somerset & Dorset Railway between Evercreech and Bath (where it would link with the Midland Railway's line to Bristol) which would have directly threatened the SCC's Radstock tramroad. The canal company, thus intimidated, decided, in August 1871, to sell the tramroad to the Somerset & Dorset. The extension opened in July 1874.

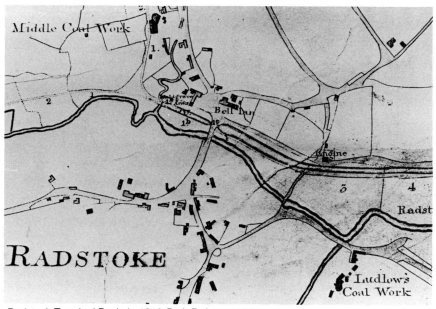

Radstock Terminal Basin in 1812. Bath Reference Library

The effect of railway competition on the SCC can be adjudged from the following tonnage receipts for coal passing through the K&A at Semington and onto the Wilts & Berks:

1854: 44,873 tons (The GWR's Frome-Radstock branch line opened)
1855: 39,003 tons
1865: 29,508 tons
1871: 19,686 tons (The Radstsock tramway was sold to the S&D)
1872: 18,037 tons
1873: 14,808 tons (The Bristol & North Somerset Railway opened)

A decade later the *total* tonnage moved on the canal had dropped to 27,724½ tons, a reduction not unaffected by the opening, in April 1882, of a 3-mile branch of the B&NSR linking Hallatrow (north-west of Paulton) with the Camerton collieries . . . though the significance of the event was seen in different terms by one anonymous local poet:

> Our coal trade will now soon revive
> There's better times for us in store
> Whilst trains continually arrive
> Close to our very door.

By 1893 the tonnage for the half year to June *along the whole length of the canal* was a mere 6,698 tons and the proprietors, at a meeting on June 14th, decided to wind up the company because of 'Bad Trade, through competition in the Coal Trade'. Trade, such as it was, continued while an Official Liquidator, charged with selling the canal as a going concern, was appointed in August the same year.

Carrying by canal was a thing of the past. A more immediate artery was in the ascendancy and, not surprisingly, no one was interested in 'the valuable freehold property', its 'nine capital stone-built cottages' nor its 'range of stone-built workshops' when it was auctioned in July 1894. The liquidator approached neighbouring railway companies and other local interests but to no avail and, with trade continuing to dwindle, it was decided that pumping should cease on November 11th 1898 and the canal close. Collieries that were still using the canal soon found alternative transport for their coal — mostly via the B&NSR's Hallatrow-Camerton branch line, thence to Bristol.

From being one of Britain's most successful canal navigations (in terms of dividends paid to shareholders), the SCC prepared to meet the dawn of a new century as little more than a derelict ditch. Ironically the less successful K&A, the mother of Britain's southern canal network, survived in GWR ownership until the 1950s and remains today as the only major man-made navigable artery in the south of England.

Why it should have been so is relatively straightforward. The SCC's *raison d'être* was Somerset's coal; other goods were carried but nothing compared in either volume or importance with the trade in coal. The railways brought with them a faster and more efficient means of getting that coal to a wider market and the collieries, despite their close connections with the Canal Company, soon took advantage. In 1871 the output of 13 collieries (on the Radstock line) was lost to the railway; in 1882 a further 75,000 tons was lost to the Camerton-Hallatrow branch line. As the SCC had no other trade to fall back on, it simply paid the price for having had all its eggs in the one basket!

Postscript

As we have seen, the SCC ceased to function as such in 1898. Subsequent events affecting the canal, the Canal Company and the Railway Companies are therefore detailed briefly below:

- 1902: Proposals were published by the North Somerset Light Railway for a line between Midford and Clutton, via Dunkerton and Camerton.
- 1903: A revised NSLR route was proposed but opposed by the GWR on the grounds that, under the terms of the Railway & Canal Traffic Act, 1888, the SCC was not yet legally abandoned. A subsequent inquiry certified the canal as derelict and confirmed its pending sale to the GWR.
- 1904: An Act confirmed the canal's abandonment and sale.
- 1907: The SCCC's affairs were finally wound up and work began on the GWR's Camerton & Limpley Stoke Railway.
- 1910: The Camerton & Limpley Stoke Railway opened for passenger and goods traffic.
- 1915: Passenger services on the Camerton & Limpley Stoke Railway ceased.
- 1951: The Camerton & Limpley Stoke Railway closed.
- 1966: The Somerset & Dorset Railway closed.

Rediscovering the Somersetshire Coal Canal

It is almost a century since the SCC saw the passage of a boat and therefore hardly surprising that its meandering course is little more than a folk-memory clinging to the shallow valleys and sleepy villages of North Somerset. In many places the chosen route of the railway devastated the line of the canal but in more recent times the tractor and the breeze block have increasingly disguised or destroyed what remains.

Nevertheless much of the canal's main line has been spared the ravages of time and man and can still be explored, albeit with a modicum of imagination . . . though, it must be said, on much of the Radstock arm even a modicum can be insufficient. Even without the canal the walks that follow offer the rambler delightful glimpses of the North Somerset landscape; the canal and railway are a bonus that punctuate the countryside with insights into an almost forgotten past.

There are eight walks altogether, five on the canal's 10½-mile Dunkerton line, three on its 7¼-mile Radstock line. All are circular, starting and finishing where there is reasonable access for the motorist and, whenever possible, those relying on public transport; details of both are given at the beginning of the text as are approximate mileages.

Being circular, the walks branch out into the canal's hinterland to return to the start by a different, often elevated, route . . . though the walker may choose to return via the outward path or combine two or more walks. Similarly, though the walks begin at the Dundas end and the SCC's junction with the K&A Canal and each proceeds in a generally south-westerly direction, they are complete in themselves and can therefore be explored in any order and in any way. On some walks the outward and return routes overlap for a short distance; there are also a few 'there and back' detours to view a particular feature.

Intrepid walkers wishing to explore the SCC as a single linear walk should note that the outward (south-westerly) route is normally closest to the original line of the canal while the return (north-easterly) route usually offers the best views across the canal and its valley.

The canal's original towpath has suffered no less at the hands of time than the canal-bed itself. Thus, more often than not, any exploration has to make use of nearby public footpaths and highways; the use of the latter is unavoidable but every effort has been made to keep it to a minimum. It can therefore be assumed that the line of the canal, even where it remains reasonably intact and enticing, must be on *private* land if it is not specifically included in the walk. None of the terrain is too demanding and, provided the walker makes allowances for seasonal weather variations and the standard of driving on footpath-less country roads, nobody should come to grief.

The Maps

Each walk is accompanied by a detailed map on which the route is highlighted by the use of bolder lines. The original line of the canal is shaded pale grey; other features are explained in the *Map Key* opposite. Numbers on the maps indicate a change of direction and correspond to a numbered description of it in the accompanying text; letters refer to features of special interest and again there is a corresponding explanation in the text. In order to make the best use of each page and to keep to the same scale throughout, all but two of the maps are read by turning the book on its side; in all cases north is towards the top of the map. Due to the recent re-routing of a small number of rights of way there may be occasional discrepancies between the accompanying maps and the appropriate OS map.

The Text

The description of each walk has three basic elements which are reinforced by the style of print in the text: changes of directions (which correspond to numbers on the map) are in bold; features of special interest (which correspond to letters on the map) are in italics; general observations, ramblings and comments are in roman. However, not every piece of protruding masonry or bend in the canal is mentioned in the text; some things have been left to the imagination while others, like the many uses local farmers have found for redundant sleepers and rails, will stir the detective in us all.

To set the scene, each walk begins with a contemporary account or recollection of a specific event or occasion from the canal's working history. For those who frequently suffer from bouts of unquenchable thirst and/or severe peckishness details of hostelries and shops conclude each walk.

Walk 2 (Midford to Combe Hay) and Walk 6 (Midford to Wellow Church) both include the same length of the Dunkerton line between Midford and Twinhoe Lane; a similar overlap is therefore reflected in the accompanying texts.

All map references are to the Ordnance Survey Pathfinder (1:25,000) series [sheets ST66/76 (1183) Bath and Keynsham and ST65/75 (1199) Radstock and Wellow].

The Photographs

Each walk is illustrated by photographs of the canal and its remains as they are today; structures that have disappeared in the recent past have been omitted even though in some cases a photographic record does exist. Hopefully the work of the Avon Industrial Buildings Trust will ensure that there are no further incursions onto the line of the canal and that existing artefacts remain in situ. On some walks where there are few remains, photographs of other interesting features of the canal's hinterland have been included.

Not all there is to know about the SCC and its industrial heritage has been unearthed; the work of AIBT and others will continue into the foreseeable future and ensure an ever-changing perspective. But whether or not these walks are the last word they will hopefully serve some small purpose if they entice the reader out into the Somerset countryside to enjoy and respect the SCC's industrial, architectural, agricultural and natural environment . . . they will have touched upon something even greater if, in addition, a little of that folk–memory rubs off and is absorbed.

MAP KEY

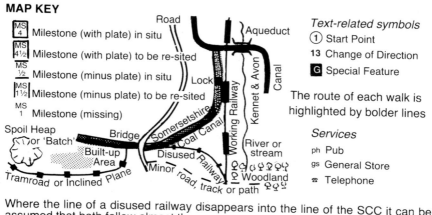

Where the line of a disused railway disappears into the line of the SCC it can be assumed that both follow almost the same course.

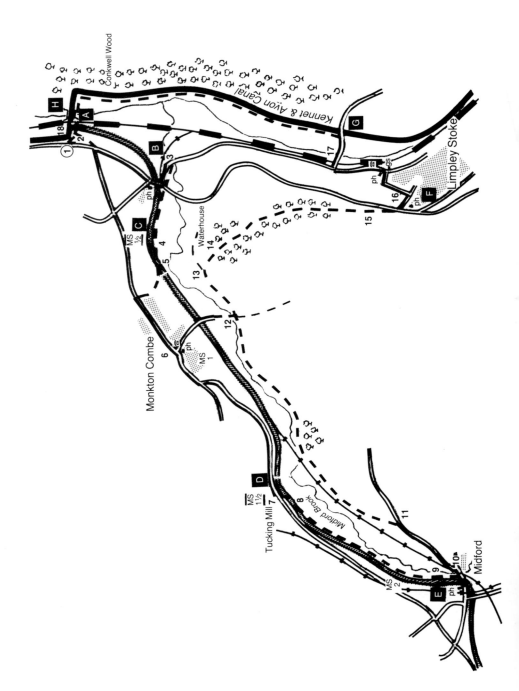

Walk 1 : Dundas Wharf to Midford.

Start Point: ST 78386253. 6 miles.

By encompassing both the SCC *and* a short stretch of the Kennet & Avon Canal this walk puts the former into its context as an arm of the latter . . . albeit an independent and important one. The scenic delights of two river valleys and the architectural splendour of Dundas Aqueduct are but icing on the cake.

Access: There is a lay-by on the main A36 just above Dundas Wharf and Aqueduct which offers adequate parking; the Bath-Trowbridge Badgerline service (265) stops at the southern end of the same lay-by; details from Bath (0225) 464446.

There was plenty of water in the lower reaches of the coal canal, and at the time it was capable of taking as full loads as at any time in its existence. The water was, I remember, remarkably clear, and freshwater fish were everywhere swimming happily about.

The lock gates seemed to be in quite good condition. The weighing machine at Midford was intact, with its ironwork looking ready to hold its boat-loads of coal, and the stone pillar supports reminded me of a Greek temple or perhaps of Pharaoh's Bed on the Island of Philae, in Egypt, but it could not have been used for a very long time, as it was standing amid a perfect bed of water-reeds.
(Sydney Bourne's recollections of traffic on the SCC in 1898 as published in Country Life, May 11th 1951.)

The lock that is not a lock at Dundas

1 Join the canal at Dundas via the flight of steps at the northern end of the A36 lay-by and head for the towpath lift-bridge that spans the entrance to the SCC.

With indecent haste time all too often weaves its destructive spell on a discarded industrial landscape. In K&A terms, Dundas Wharf has suffered less than most such sites, likewise the entrance lock and adjacent lock-keeper's cottage of the SCC. Sadly, the same cannot be said of the original stone towpath bridge which, even when the K&A was still a working waterway, was levelled to fill in the old canal entrance. However, today's pleasure boating boom has brought new life to this end of the SCC and though the new aluminium lift-bridge barely stands comparison with the humped back of the original stone incumbent, its very presence and the restoration of the adjacent lock chamber have created interest anew in the canal. Of course the only similarity between the boats that now pass through the lock to and from the security of their moorings and their predecessors is that they are narrow-beamed though, it must be said, such ambassadors of the pleasure industry are sustaining an important tradition of trade on the canal . . . the carrying of people.

A Over the years the ENTRANCE LOCK to the SCC has witnessed several important changes to its original concept. When the canal was built, this lock, unlike the rest of the canal, was built broad — presumably to accommodate the wider barges of the K&A. Although the SCC was conceived as a narrow canal, in 1800 Benjamin Outram had suggested, as part of the report on his Inclined Plane proposals, that the lower level of both lines be widened to about three-quarters of a mile west of Midford. Recent excavation of the entrance lock has confirmed that it was originally built broad which supports the local tradition that barges from the K&A traded up the canal as far as Tucking Mill. Whether or not this was some sort of half-hearted response to Outram's ideas is not known; what is more certain is that by around 1820 the lock had been
narrowed to exclude wider craft and Dundas Wharf established as a gauging station for traffic from the SCC. Canal company rivalries probably fuelled the reasoning behind such a drastic change though there could have been little financial benefit to carriers working barges up the canal so far . . . but no further. Of some, though admittedly small, advantage to the SCC would have been the saving of water each time a boat worked through as there was a difference of 7in (in the SCC's favour) between the normal levels of the two canals. And it is here that the re-use of this end of the canal has brought with it another change — the entrance lock is now no more than a gate-less narrow chamber, its duties as a so-called stop-lock having found no place in the new order of things.

2 Take the path that climbs almost parallel to the canal from Dundas Wharf to the A36 and turn left onto the main road; follow the footpath to the traffic lights opposite the *Viaduct Hotel* and turn left towards Limpley Stoke.

It is perhaps ironic that the sole navigable section of the SCC is also the only part beside which it is not normally possible to walk as the towpath alongside the Bath & Dundas Canal Company's moorings is off-limits to all but berth-holders and hirers except at weekends and bank holidays when the premises can be entered through the double gate on the K&A towpath right beside Dundas Aqueduct. Nevertheless the walk up to the A36 offers intermittent views of the canal, its new clientele and, across the valley, the line of the Kennet & Avon. Water now extends right up to the A36 for here is the quaintly named Brass Knocker Bottom boatyard. The visitor centre is open for boat hire and enquiries, ice creams and drinks, all week in summer. Access is off the B3108 to Limpley Stoke. The SCC crosses under the A36 just east of the traffic lights, its line all the easier to pick out now that boat moorings have been extended.

3 Turn sharp right onto the designated path at the first right-hand bend along the Limpley Stoke road and continue under the A36

viaduct and alongside the playing fields of Monkton Combe School.

B   Although the line of the GWR's CAMERTON & LIMPLEY STOKE RAILWAY (the metalled track above the path but below the canal) destroyed part of the canal embankment west of the Viaduct Hotel, the two clearly do not follow the same line. Both did, of course, follow the Midford Brook valley but, here as elsewhere, it would be wrong to assume that in doing so the railway stuck religiously to the same route as the canal . . . only just over 20% of the canal between Dundas and Timsbury Basin was destroyed by the railway. Nevertheless, here the railway, itself a victim of time and expediency, remains the more clearly defined as its embankment, less dependent on contours, takes a more direct line towards Midford . . . thus foregoing any acquiescence to the demand for tennis courts hereabouts.

C   As on other canals, MILESTONES on the SCC were a statutory requirement as the basis for calculating tolls. Styles and materials varied from one canal to another and sometimes even along the same canal while some, like road-side milestones, gave distances to and from two locations. On the main line of the SCC there were 21 milestones, solid stone slabs with an inset brass plate, indicating distances at ½-mile intervals to the K&A at Dundas. Only 10 remain in situ and of these a mere two retain their plates; unfortunately many, including these two, are not visible from public footpaths and roads. One that falls into this category is the ½-milestone between Dundas and Monkton Combe; a lone and inaccessible sentinel, defiantly it stands its ground amid the overgrown remains of the canal bank.

4   Veer right from the playing fields and up the gently sloping path to the school road; turn left and, 20 yards on, left again towards the pavilion then immediately right onto the path that runs above and parallel to the road.

5   Cross the road where the path peters out and continue up the grassy hill towards the school buildings, passing to the right of these to join the road to Monkton Combe; turn left onto the road.

The line of the canal remains intact for a short distance between the path and the track (the railway) just east of where the two cross; at the site of their 'union'

The 1½-milestone in front of the 'wrong' cottage

stood a cast-iron bridge that carried the path to Monkton Combe. The bridge which bore a plate indicating that it was CAST AT PAULTON 1811, survived to serve both canal and railway ... albeit aided and abetted by two brick pillars to facilitate the age of steam. The lines of both canal and railway pass south of Monkton Combe School and are generally inaccessible; not so the village described by Arthur Mee as 'down a hill to paradise, down into one of those beautiful hollows which make the country round Bath like a little Switzerland' ... and not a mention of the Wheelwright's Arms!

6 Remain on the road through Monkton Combe (it turns sharp right and then left round the church) and turn left off the Combe Down road following the sign to Tucking Mill and Midford.

Down in the valley the line of the canal and railway remain as an almost-healed scar ... only the line of the canal embankment survives as if to haunt its erstwhile rival. As the road bends round to the right so too the canal parts company with the railway and swings north-west towards Tucking Mill and a stone arch bridge (originally a draw-bridge) that remains intact but hidden from view.

7 Turn left onto the overgrown path just beyond Tucking Mill Cottage and the new Bath-stone garages and cross the stile; stop to look at William Smith's cottage across the road to the right.

D The names of WILLIAM SMITH and TUCKING MILL seem almost synonymous though the latter survives only as a geographical location. The original mill was once part of the prosperous local woollen industry and its replacement saw the canal come and go before surrendering to the ravages of time in 1927. William Smith was one of the surveyors associated with the canal from 1794 but while supervising construction work and purchasing land locally he acquired a cottage near the mill as a private residence and with it the wrath of the SCC committee. His subsequent

dismissal in April 1799 was, seemingly, a direct result of this abuse of his position. That said, it is difficult to escape the conclusion that he must also have incurred the committee's displeasure in other areas and that they merely used this as an excuse to terminate his employment. The SCC's loss was geology's gain for Smith went on to greater things (he established the principles of rock stratification and identification by fossil contents) culminating in the siting of a plaque, in 1888, on the wrong cottage at Tucking Mill!

HERE LIVED
WILLIAM SMITH
'FATHER OF ENGLISH GEOLOGY'
BORN 23RD MARCH 1769
DIED 28TH AUGUST 1839

Though 'Strata Smith' only resided in the area for a short time he did establish a tramway down the hill (and past his cottage) from stone quarries to a canalside wharf by Tucking Mill — a trade that probably finished when the lock at Dundas was narrowed and barges could no longer use the canal.

8 Follow the path across the line of the canal bed; it crosses and recrosses for a time before settling on the southern side of the canal ditch.

The railway embankment that soon looms large and almost cliff-like to the north was once the Somerset & Dorset Joint Railway; the Camerton & Limpley Stoke line is the lower embankment beyond Midford Brook to the south. Both railways, the brook and the canal converge at Midford and, not surprisingly, it is the latter that has suffered most from the resulting congestion.

9 Just north of Midford follow the path as it deviates to the left around a private garden and join the main road; turn right to view the overgrown bed of the canal by the Hope and Anchor.

E MIDFORD WEIGH-HOUSE, the 'Greek Temple' that so impressed the young Sydney Bourne in 1898, was demolished during the Great War; what little remains to identify the site and its short arm of canal lie hidden in the garden of Lynwood House. Completed in 1831, the boat weighing machine accurately recorded a cargo's weight as a means of calculating tolls. The weight of each unladen boat using the canal would be known and on any subsequent loaded passage the boat would enter the weighing machine 'lock' to be left suspended on cradlelike scales when the water was drained off. Although the Thames & Severn and the Glamorganshire Canals also boasted such contrivances, neither seems to have been so ornately disguised as their precursor here at Midford. In its first year of operation the Thames & Severn model recouped more than its capital cost in tolls from undisclosed cargo – as it post-dates the one at Midford by some 15 years, it can be assumed that the SCC had gained similar advantages.

The blocked-off northern face of the road tunnel at Midford can be viewed from the bridge parapet but the fireside window of the adjacent *Hope and Anchor* offers a warmer and more refreshing aspect. The pub's beer garden also looks out onto the canal to where boats and their thirsty crews once enjoyed the inn's hospitality before and after negotiating the nearby weighing machine. In its name, Moorings, the house across the road from the pub retains a little of its canal connections . . . it was the original toll collector's house.

10   About turn and head east along the main road past the path back to Tucking Mill; turn left into Midford Lane and Wiltshire (just beyond the C&LSR viaduct).

11   About 300 yards further on, Midford Lane veers to the right; take the path here across the stile to the left and continue north-east diagonally across the field and eventually through a gap in the stone wall.

The track is but one of several routes taking advantage of the valley. Between it and Midford Brook is the C&LSR track bed while the line of trees beyond harbours the remains of the

canal. Above and behind is the lofty embankment of the S&DJR and overlooking it all the castellated façade of Midford Castle. Tucking Mill and William Smith's house soon dominate the view across the valley to where the curve of the canal is given a new perspective. Hidden among the trees a little further on is the south-west abutment of the erstwhile C&LSR viaduct across Midford Brook; it was just east of here that the canal and railway became almost as one.

12   Several stiles and fields later the path crosses Mill Lane via a stile and a flight of stone steps; turn left initially and walk up towards Monkton Combe to where the line of the canal and railway clearly cross at the garden of Appledore; return to the steps and turn left.

Not surprisingly, Mill Lane passes alongside a mill which, although redundant, still manages to evoke memories of more prosperous times . . . perhaps it's no more than an illusion created by the sound of the river and its mill race and the expectant stance of the sluices. Or perhaps it's just that, compared with the canal just up the hill, there's a lot more to see, for not only has the canal succumbed to the railway but the site of Monkton Combe Station has itself given way to tennis courts. Needless to say, of the stone-arch bridge that once stood here, there is nothing to trace!

13   Continue along the river-side path which soon turns sharp right and then left up the hill; turn right off the lane where it joins with the track up to Brett Farm and climb the steps to cross the stile.

14   Strike diagonally left up the field to the stile in the far fence; cross this and follow the well-defined path round the wooded hillside.

The climb up the hill and round towards Limpley Stoke offers excellent views down to the line of the canal between Monkton Combe and the A36. The *Viaduct Hotel*, it seems, is an ever-present landmark around which road, river, railway and canal can all be given their rightful place. As the climb steepens, the trees close in as if to deliberately obscure the change in scenery and prepare the unsuspecting walker for the rush and roar of the increasingly intrusive A36.

15 Where the path appears to go through a gate keep left down the narrow path to the A36; carefully cross the A36 and continue down Woods Hill opposite into Limpley Stoke.

16 Take the first left off Woods Hill, following the road down and round to the right to the T-junction at the bottom; turn left out of Limpley Stoke and right at the next T-junction.

F LIMPLEY STOKE is a sleepy little village that nestles in the wooded valley of the Avon. Despite the proximity of the A36, time seems to have almost stopped here ... hardly the sort of place that would have given its name to a railway! Although it was in February 1951 that the last train from Monkton Combe steamed into Limpley Stoke, the following summer brought a new lease of life to the defunct branch-line and its environs in the shape of The Titfield Thunderbolt. *Valley and railway were enlivened by the excitement generated by a busy film crew and their 'star'* Lion, *the 'Titfield Thunderbolt'. Each evening* Lion *was stabled in a siding here at Limpley Stoke while the adjacent river-side mill became a makeshift projection room for viewing the day's filming. The mill's old waterwheel provided the power and inspired one wit to label this new local cinema* Hydr-O-Deon!

17 Climb the hill under the railway, over the river to join the K&A by turning left before the bridge and immediately right onto the towpath; turn left and head north towards Dundas Aqueduct and Wharf.

G LIMPLEY STOKE BRIDGE is scarcely different to any other K&A canal bridge except that in restoration terms it has, in recent years, become a line of demarcation between puddle clay and concrete. Canals are normally rendered watertight by a thick layer of puddle clay but ever since the K&A was built the section between Limpley Stoke and Avoncliff has been especially prone to 'blow-outs'. It was therefore decided that, as part of the Kennet & Avon Canal Trust's restoration programme, this length should be permanently secured with a concrete bed. The work was completed in 1978, since when what had become known euphemistically as the 'dry section' has successfully retained its water.

The walk along the K&A back to Dundas is full of interest, not least because once again the canal is enjoying the passage of boats which, if nothing else, helps recreate an image of what it must have been like on the SCC. In addition to the natural splendours of the Limpley Stoke valley, there are mileposts, stop-gates and plug winches (rollers that were once connected to a chain and plug on the canal bed) and occasional glimpses of the strong lines of Dundas Aqueduct. There are more frequent views across the Avon and its confluence with Midford Brook to the SCC embankment and the line of boats already encountered at the beginning of the walk. Just before the bend east of the aqueduct is what was a lengthsman's cottage and the remains of stables that probably sheltered horses used on the SCC. On the far bank, in the shadow of Conkwell Wood, there was once a wharf served by a tramroad from Conkwell Quarry above; for a time the stone from here was used in the construction of the canal but because of its inferior quality, quarrying was soon discontinued. On the bend itself look out too for the corner post which prevented tow ropes from cutting across the corner and pulling the boat round sideways. Apart from the plug winches (which were unique to the Kennet & Avon and Chesterfield Canals) all these features would have had SCC equivalents, albeit to a smaller scale ... that said, the splendour of Dundas Aqueduct has almost no equal!

Finally, although this book is about the SCC it must be remembered that it only existed and functioned successfully because of the K&A. The craft that carried coal from the collieries on the Dunkerton and Radstock lines also plied these waters and were as much affected by, for example, the vicissitudes of the 'dry section' as were the K&A's barges.

H   DUNDAS AQUEDUCT is one of two aqueducts that carry the K&A across the Avon valley. Though shorter than Avoncliff to the south-east, the setting is more dramatic, its doric columns, despite the effect of time and weather on the downstream face, totally at one with their environment. Dundas and Avoncliff were the audacious creation of the canal's engineer, John Rennie, and though his skills as such have often been held suspect, the architectural magnificence of his aqueducts remain as bold testimonies to his imagination.

Beyond the aqueduct is Dundas Basin and Wharf, their redundant crane, warehouse and toll-office overseeing a scene transformed by the sights and sounds of pleasure boats and boaters. These in turn have brought others to the canal to walk and talk and recreate in the mind's eye a time almost forgotten. In the recent re-opening of the entrance lock and the moorings beyond, the long-lost SCC is playing a small part in piecing together the story and the feel of what was, in its heyday, a new and exciting adventure into the unknown.

18 Return to the A36 via the steps at the back of Dundas Wharf.

SHOPS: Life-saving Yorkie bars and other goodies can be purchased at Limpley Stoke Post Office and General Stores, apart from the boatyard, the only shop en route.

SUSTENANCE: Pubs-wise this is undoubtedly the best walk! There are five altogether: The *Viaduct Hotel* (Courage) near Dundas and the *Wheelwright's Arms* (Whitbread) at Monkton Combe (both of which offer B&B), the *Hope and Anchor* (Free House) at Midford, the *Rose and Crown* (Courage) and the *Hop Pole* (Courage) at Limpley Stoke; all do excellent food, so *Nightingales*, the restaurant by the river at Limpley Stoke, is but a bonus.

A culvert under the canal between Tucking Mill and Midford, probably a drainage sluice

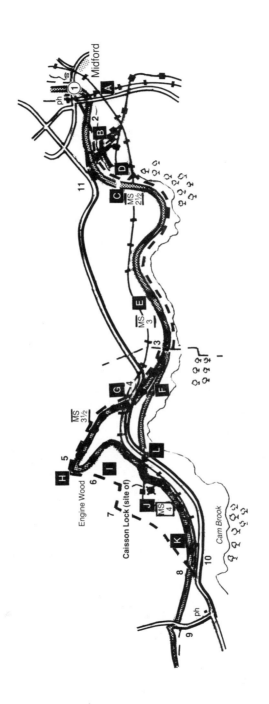

Midford

ph

① A

2

B

C D

MS 2½

3

E MS 3

G 4

F

MS 3½ H 5

Engine Wood I 6

7 J MS 4

Caisson Lock (site of) K

8

9 ph

10

L

Cam Brook

11

Walk 2 : Midford to Combe Hay.

Start Point: ST 76076063. 4½ miles.

Though shorter than the other walks, the canal's line from Midford to Combe Hay is arguably not only the most interesting but also the best preserved and most accessible. The locks, the inclined plane and the caisson are, of course, the star attractions though only the former leaves little to the imagination.

Access: Parking on main-road Midford is not advised – the road signposted to Twinhoe offers safer possibilities. On the other hand patrons of the *Hope and Anchor* may use its car park but should seek out the landlord and let him know. Besides the obvious, the pub is a good starting point for, as we have seen (Walk 1), its fireside window looks out onto the northern face of the canal bridge. Midford is on Badgerline's infrequent Frome-Bath-Bristol Swiftlink service (X3); details from Bath (0225) 464446 or Bristol (0272) 553231.

> Saturday afternoon, as a lad, engaged in a barge from Devizes, was winding a windlass to let the water through the locks, near Combhay [*sic*], he lost his balance and fell in; he was not missed for a space of 4 or 5 minutes when, in apprehending some accident caused by his absence, the bargemen dragged the water and found the body with life extinct.
>
> (*Extract from the Bath Chronicle, October 14th 1830*)

A refurbished lock at Combe Hay

1 Leave the main road at Midford via the signposted path opposite the *Hope and Anchor*; the path soon changes from one side of the canal to the other via a stile.

The southern parapet of the road bridge over the canal remains visible though only as a decorative part of a long ornamental garden that was originally the canal bed. Looming larger above are the Somerset & Dorset Railway viaduct and the road to Twinhoe before; at the end of the garden a short overgrown stretch opens out into one of the best preserved lengths of canal.

A It was the sale of the Radstock Tramway to the SOMERSET & DORSET RAILWAY in 1871 that was effectively the beginning of the end of the SCC. The 8-arched brick and stone viaduct here at Midford was clearly one of the railway's major engineering works and one that, as reported by the Bath Chronicle *in August 1872, was soon far advanced:*

> *The large viaduct over the ponds at Midford is in a very forward state, both abutments and two piers being ready for the arches and three-quarters of the remaining piers are completed.*

When the railway opened in July 1874 it linked Radstock and its hinterland of coalfields with the Midland Railway at Bath and in doing so emphasised all the more the deficiencies of its northern rival, the Dunkerton line of the canal.

B The short 3-arched stone span of MIDFORD AQUEDUCT sits astride the Cam Brook at the northern end of the Radstock branch at its junction with the canal's main line. Much of the Bath stone has suffered with time — particularly the western face — but the aqueduct remains as a robust testimony to the hopes that once fired those that planned a working waterway between here and Radstock. The eastern face of the main arch (there were two flood arches) still bears an inscribed stone panel, its lettering worn with age:

> MITFORD
> AQUÆDUCT
> ERECTED
> 18   03
> R. TYLER

Beyond the aqueduct there was probably initially only a single channel — the chamber of the one lock that was actually completed — which was used as a transhipment point for the 'temporary' tramroad from Twinhoe. With the construction of a tramway throughout in 1815 this was extended to form a much larger basin, its wharves, sidings and buildings geared to coping with the increase in trade from the Radstock collieries. Thus, from 1815 until the sale of the Radstock Tramway in 1871, Midford Aqueduct and its hinterland of wharves was the only part of the SCC's route to Radstock that was actually in water.

The public footpath from Midford has kept generally to the south of the canal but between Midford and the entrance of the Radstock arm there was a towing path on both sides, there being no bridge across the entrance. Craft using the Dunkerton line were re-united with the southern towpath via the stone accommodation bridge at Upper Midford.

C The TURNOVER BRIDGE here started life as a necessity to comply with the legal requirement embodied in all canal Acts that the lines of existing highways be preserved. Thus, when the lane between Upper Midford and Twinhoe was bisected by the canal, an appropriate crossing had to be provided. The kind of bridge depended on the volume and type of traffic though generally speaking canal companies honed in on the cheapest option, normally some kind of movable bridge. Between the junction of the canal's two lines and Midford there were, seemingly, towing paths on both sides of the canal — the southern one for traffic using the Radstock arm, the northern one for boats using the Dunkerton line. It was here at Upper Midford that traffic on the latter 'turned over' to and from the northern path.

2 Cross the stile just to the south of the bridge and turn left to follow the

path under an arch of the C&LSR viaduct; on the other side cross the next stile off to the left to rejoin the canal-side path.

D   Canal companies sited BOUNDARY POSTS, such as the two either side of the canal just south of the stone bridge, to indicate the limits of their property. As with mileposts these varied in style between one canal and another, those on the SCC being stone and bearing the letters CCC (Coal Canal Company).

Though the path passes round the railway viaduct, it is possible to scramble up the viaduct's embankment to look down on the canal as, on the one hand, it sweeps gently south and, on the other, it curves sharply under the stone turnover bridge towards Midford Aqueduct. Just below the viaduct, on the canal's south-west embankment, the top of a stone milepost protrudes from the ground; its plate, no longer in situ, indicated that Dundas was 2½ miles away. The viaduct itself is worthy of more than a backward glance . . . the railway may appear to be going in a different direction but before long its embankment all but crosses the canal. In between, at the apex of the canal's loop to the south, a low mound extends out from the embankment into the adjacent field. A recent accidental 'excavation' of the mound revealed fragments of china, glass and clay pipes, the shells of oysters, cockles and mussels and coal and coke ashes which suggests that it might have been a tip set aside for canal boatmen and their families . . . a theory given credence by an early OS map that marks the site with two boundary posts.

E   The decaying remains of LOCK 22, the first of the Combe Hay flight, lurk in the undergrowth almost opposite the small bridge over the Cam Brook. Originally this and the next two were part of the 3-lock flight that obviated the need for a deep cutting further on at the Feeder Cut, the approach to Jessop's inclined plane; they therefore pre-date the rest of the locks by several years. But like the rest they were to the standard narrow-gauge pattern familiar on other canals; 75ft long, 7ft wide, a rise/fall of 6ft regulated by ground

paddles, a single top gate and two mitred bottom gates. The chambers of locks 21 and 20 are easy to find but have suffered no less than their neighbour at the rampant hands of the encroaching vegetation.

3   Cross the stile and turn right into the old pack-horse lane from South Stoke to Upper Twinhoe; a few yards on turn left off the lane by crossing another stile.

A   stone   accommodation   bridge originally crossed the canal here as evidenced by a few fragments of the north-east wing parapet. Beyond the bridge there are two distinctly separate lengths of canal, the more northerly line to the rest of the Combe Hay locks and the southern ditch that led to the inclined plane, the short-lived Feeder Cut.

F   Although the line of the FEEDER CUT crosses private property, there is no such restriction to the imagination . . . provided, of course, it can leap the 40 yards or so beyond Twinhoe Lane and south of the overgrown footpath to the junction with the rest of the lock flight. Beyond the junction, locks 19, 18 and 17 ran north-west in a line parallel to the Feeder until the back of Bridge

A Coal Canal Company boundary post

Farm (the site of the lock-keeper's and lengthsman's cottages) where the latter took a more westerly course to its terminal basin below the inclined plane – the line of which is crossed later in the walk. After the completion of the lock flight in 1805 the Feeder Cut was abandoned although its basin was retained as a reservoir for the lower level of the canal.

4 Cross another stile and follow the more open path to the back of Bridge Farm; bear right here, cross the stile, the main road and the stile directly opposite (just beyond the railway viaduct) and follow the path uphill alongside the locks.

G The climb up the hillside from LOCK 15 (lock 16 disappeared under the railway embankment) is one of sensory contrasts. On the one hand the wooded setting is glorious, on the other the partially restored locks punctuate the hillside as defiant reminders of a way of life long past . . . a way of life that, even in such surroundings, claimed the life of the young lad 'engaged in a barge from Devizes'. The locks and their environs have been snatched from further decay by the Avon Industrial

Buildings Trust which, since 1984, has sought to preserve and restore the chambers and open up the site to a wider public. A milepost stands in situ by Lock 13 and though its plate is gone it seems more at home than the wayward tree jutting arrogantly out of the stonework; both are 3½ miles from Dundas.

H The approach to the BULL'S NOSE, the name given to the hairpin bend between locks 11 and 10, is soon complemented on the left by the line of locks continuing on up the hill. The bend itself looks as tight as any on the canal network and must have been difficult to negotiate particularly when boats were passing. Local lore has it that there was also a small wharf here that served the nearby fuller's earth mines.

5 Cross the stile above Lock 11 and follow the path along the apex of the bend and uphill to the left through Engine Wood.

From the Bull's Nose the view down and up the locks is unusual to say the least; it is one too that should be savoured, for the path up through

The western façade of Midford Aqueduct

Engine Wood diverges from the canal, giving only a glimpse of Lock 9. Sadly, for the moment, the remaining eight locks are for the imagination only.

I *Engine Wood housed COMBE HAY ENGINE HOUSE that, from early 1806, pumped water that had passed through the locks back up to the head of the flight. A feeder was cut from the pumping station to the inclined plane's terminal basin which in turn connected with the pound above Lock 1. During the 1840s the pumping engine was removed to Dunkerton and the house itself demolished in the 1870s, though some of its foundations remain visible close to the path which for a time follows the line of the feeder ditch.*

6 At the southern end of Engine Wood follow the path over the stile and right onto the track; cross the next stile and field towards the stile opposite.

J *Somewhere hereabouts lurk the remains of CAISSON LOCK . . . that much is known! Robert Weldon's amazing Hydrostatick or Caisson Lock was one of the wonders of the Canal Age. Its short-lived trials and tribulations captured the imagination of anyone and everyone who heard of it and yet, like some seven-day wonder, its massive bulk was soon redundant and forgotten, consumed by the earth and banished to the indignity of an unmarked grave. Various theories have been put forward as to the location of the 81ft × 16½ft × 20ft stone cistern and its wooden caisson – such a bulk would have, it was assumed, left some trace. Some of the theories have been followed up with excavations but nothing directly connected with the caisson has ever been unearthed. However, Hugh Torrens' researches, published in BIAS (the journal of the Bristol Industrial Archaeological Society) in 1975, seem to have settled the matter . . . albeit without any excavatory evidence. Torrens looked at the facts through four different lines of enquiry – the Smith-Carey map of 1796, the geological structure of the area, Bath Reference Library's 1810 map and other written evidence – all four lines intersected in the same area.*

In 1876 Bath bookseller and publisher, R E M Peach, revised James Tunstall's Rambles about Bath and its Neighbourhood and added the following to Tunstall's description of Combe Hay: 'The situation [of the Caisson Lock] is close to the residence of Mr Hill the Engineer of the Canal Company and the lower end of the chamber is marked by a tree planted by Mr Hill's father. The drop was sixty feet and the walls are believed to be still perfect when filled up.' The lines of Torrens' research converge by an artificial-looking mound between Caisson House (Hill's residence) and Lock 5. The mound, crowned by an old chestnut tree, is, sadly not part of this walk . . . but then it doesn't really matter, for the caisson is interred forever in the imagination which, for those who want to know more, can be fed further by reference to Appendix A.

7 Cross the stile at the top of the field, turn left along the edge of the next towards the stile and the farm buildings; keep these on the right and head down to the main road.

For some it may be frustrating to think that just over the fence, within and around Caisson Field, there is so much more to see – the site of the reservoir that probably fed the caisson, Caisson House itself, the terminal basin for the inclined plane, a stone bridge, locks a-plenty, a milestone with its plate and, of course, a chestnut tree. Frustrating it may be, but life goes on around these gentle slopes and for the people who live and work hereabouts a bevy of intrepid caisson-hunters could be more than a little inconvenience. Suffice to know that what is left will remain intact and even that a minor mystery might remain unresolved.

K *The SUMMIT JUNCTION between the feeder from Engine Wood (part of which was the original arm to the inclined plane's summit level) and the head of Lock 1 lies about 35 yards to the east of the entrance to Rowley Farm and Caisson House. Originally a swivel bridge assured access to both across the canal; its replacement, the more familiar stone bridge, has also gone. A glimpse of the canal's line* towards the junction can be snatched from behind the hedge at the right of the driveway entrance to Caisson House. A canal's summit level (in the SCC's case the length from Timsbury Basin to Lock 1) is like a linear reservoir which, with every lock-full of water that is drawn off, requires topping up. Water-supply was, on the SCC and almost every other canal, a perennial problem to canal engineers and administrators. During the summer of 1870, for example, a system of 'waiting turns' (boats working up having to wait for one to work down before passing through, and vice versa) was introduced on the Combe Hay flight to save water . . . a restriction that one boatman, Edmund Ettel, flaunted when he 'took a marling-spike and broke the padlock by which the lock was fastened and then passed through'.

A little further down the hill another bridge remains virtually intact and in a deep cutting below is the track-less bed of the railway. About 100 yards to the west the railway and canal cross and, not surprisingly, the line of the latter is the worse for the encounter. It is worth recalling that the two met just opposite

Bridge Farm; then the railway crossed high above the infilled chamber of Lock 16; now, 15 locks later, the positions are reversed.

8 Turn right onto the Combe Hay-Midford road towards Combe Hay; take the next right by the Wheatsheaf and continue uphill to the site of the canal bridge.

The last view of the canal is of an overgrown, though reasonably well-defined, ditch to the west of the lane which, like so many other canal/road encounters, has lost both its original swivel bridge and its stone arch replacement. For many years a second plate-adorned milestone (4½ miles from Dundas) stood a few hundred yards to the west but, though it has gone, it has been preserved and hopefully will be re-erected in a more public place.

9 Return to the main road, turn left and head back towards Midford.

It is the railway cutting to the left that dominates much of the early part of the walk back to Midford, though the canal

The Bull's Nose

and its locks run parallel in the field beyond. On the right is a house, Inner Meadow, that is also known locally as Platform Cottage. This stands about 75 yards uphill from the junction of the Feeder Cut and the inclined plane and was thus probably the original wharfinger's house. From the road the knowing eye can pick up occasional glimpses of the line of the Feeder Cut down in the valley below.

L   The line of the INCLINED PLANE crossed the Midford road here and continued up the hill opposite to a point near the southern end of Caisson House. The plane was some 300 yards long, connecting the upper and lower basins with a rise/fall of 115ft. In canal terms there were basically two kinds of plane – those that transferred the cargo between two levels and those that transferred the boat and its cargo. Here at Combe Hay it was the former version that for four years (1801–1805) provided the link between the lower level of the canal and its summit level.

Before the days of the railway the road and the locks were linked by a track just off to the left between the plane and Bridge Farm. For the boatmen this was no ordinary link with civilization but rather a short cut down to the Anchor Inn that once stood here. At Bridge Farm it is certainly tempting to turn right and return to Midford via the canal as it is, a little further on, at Twinhoe Lane. The choice is the walker's but it is often worthwhile to look at the canal and its environs from a different perspective . . . even if it does mean coping with the hazards of a footpath-less country road.

10   Remain on the Midford road as far as the Hyver Kennels and rejoin the canal by turning right off the road via the signposted path just beyond.

Local tradition has it that the Hyver Kennels was originally the Boatman's Arms which, needless to say, was oft frequented by passing boatmen. Today canal-side pubs are in; they meet the modern need for comfort and relaxation in an out-of-town setting. For the working boatman they were an integral part of his day-to-day routines and were

often built by or on land owned by the canal company. Many were no more than ale-houses that provided relaxation and a good stable while others were regular meeting places for boatmen and their families. It is not surprising therefore that a pub should have flourished here by the junction of the two arms of the canal . . . even less surprising that both canal and pub have long gone.

11   Turn left onto the north side of the canal embankment and then cross the canal bed at a point just opposite Midford Aqueduct where there is a gap in the old canal retaining wall; return to Midford via the canalside path.

With the walk amost complete, it is worth remembering that this waterless ditch was not only the domain of boats and boatmen but was also the natural habitat of a variety of flora and fauna. A South Stoke vicar once wrote of the Combe Hay locks as follows: 'In these basins many an uncommon and beautiful flower grew, especially when its banks were clothed in summer time with the flowering rush Butomus umbellatus, one of the most beautiful of our English wild flowers. The water being clear and limpid, many species of fresh-water algae could be observed, and such fish as roach and perch could be seen in the clear water and maybe a pike lying silently as if carved in stone, by the side of some water-weed . . . I have never known gudgeon inhabit canal water, yet here they were to be found . . . It is a fish that delights in clear and running water and by no means an inhabitant of ponds and canals.'

SHOPS: Stock up before setting off – there are no shops en route!

SUSTENANCE: Both the Hope and Anchor (Free House) and the Wheatsheaf (Courage) at Combe Hay do excellent food and it is possible to have a lunchtime drink in both on the same walk; the latter also offers accommodation.

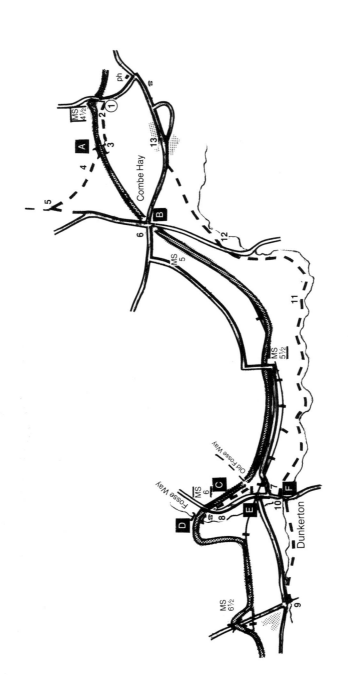

Walk 3 : Combe Hay to Dunkerton.

Start Point: ST 73556014. 5 miles.

Thanks to the architects of the Camerton & Limpley Stoke Railway, there are fewer glimpses of the canal on this walk than any other on the Dunkerton line. Roads and footpaths are also something of a problem but nevertheless there are a few unexpected surprises including two aqueducts and a tunnel.

Access: It is possible to park on the lane close to Combe Hay Cemetery but the *Wheatsheaf* car park is clearly more suitable. Not surprisingly, this facility is made available to patrons who, in any case should seek out the landlord and obtain permission. There is no bus service to the Combe Hay area but those relying on public transport could start and finish at Dunkerton (direction 7) where several Badgerline services link with Bath and one with Bristol; details from Bath (0225) 464446 or Bristol (0272) 553231.

> . . . 24 boats built for conveyance of materials on the Somerset Coal Canal, 13 of which are square ends, 23ft in length, 6½ft wide and 4ft deep, with elm bottoms and deal ends and sides. Others built of oak, pointed ends, and from 20-30ft in length. Boats in good condition and 2 entirely new. May be viewed at the Company's wharf at Dunkerton.
> *(Advertisement in the Bath Chronicle, January 10th 1803)*

The northern portal of
Combe Hay Tunnel

33

1 Cross the stile on the left at the southern end of Combe Hay Cemetery and where the path levels out turn left down the steps to cross the stile at the bottom.

2 Turn right along the edge of the field towards another stile; cross this and follow the overgrown path to the next stile beyond which path and stream virtually become one.

On the right is the canal/railway embankment for at this point – and for some distance to come – they are almost as one, or rather the railway has all but taken over the canal bed. The stream that rushes along on the left flows down from Fortnight Farm, under the canal and into the Cam Brook near Combe Hay.

3 Step across the stream and follow it under the canal and railway, keeping to the flagstones alongside.

A   COMBE HAY AQUEDUCT, which bears more resemblance to a culvert, was originally only some 30ft wide as evidenced by the distinctly different construction of part of the roof. It was extended in brick to its present length of 110ft to facilitate the railway. The unusual flagstone path underneath and alongside the stream was laid to maintain it as a right of way.

4 At the far end of the 'tunnel' cross the stream and follow the path up the field keeping the stream on the left; head for the stile onto the track by the house.

Don't forget to cast a glance back at the aqueduct and the high railway embankment; clearly the canal embankment would have been narrower but it was also taller for the C&LSR had to lower the canal bed to facilitate their track. While pondering the aqueduct and its embankment don't miss the old, gnarled stump of a tree that stands impervious to time and tide in the middle of the field. The stream that has its origins in a spring at Fortnight Farm also passes Week Farm and, where the path joins the main road, a house called Three Days . . . not many people will know that!

5 Cross the stile and turn left onto the track and continue down the hill where this joins the main road to Combe Hay.

From the track there are further views east across to Combe Hay Aqueduct and the tree-topped embankment above as it sweeps south-west towards Combe Hay. Just before and opposite the north-west parapet of Combe Hay Tunnel is Tunnel House which may have had some connection with the canal.

B   The 195½ft COMBE HAY TUNNEL cuts under the crossroads at Combe Hay diagonally. Rennie's original survey of the canal's route envisaged a much longer tunnel (¾-mile) here but he had second thoughts on this (just as he had about Bruce Tunnel on the Kennet & Avon) and alterations were made that took the canal to a higher level. The tunnel had a towing path along its southern side and a height above water-level of between 7ft 7in and 11ft 9in. The north-eastern parapet can be viewed by leaving the roadway via the gap in the fence at its southern end (the Midford road) and scrambling down the bank . . . though, of course, the tunnel was widened and deepened by the C&LSR.

6 Turn right at Combe Hay crossroads and take the first left, remaining on the road as far as the main A367 at Dunkerton.

The western face of Combe Hay Tunnel can be glimpsed by the long-necked from a gap in the fence just beyond its parapet; thereafter gaps in the hedge offer occasional sights of the embankment though these are more frequent after the left-hand turn. Rev John Skinner, the Rector of Camerton, wrote in his diary in January 1823, '. . . the boys wished me to accompany them to skaite, I walked with them to the Dundas Aqueduct in Claverton valley, and skaited for four hours on a fine piece of ice where the Combe Hay canal had not been broken.' Looking down into the valley is it just possible to glimpse a swirling black cassock frolicking under a hazy sun and pick up the sound of high-spirited laughter as

The northern façade of Dunkerton Aqueduct

the mind's eye re-creates that wintry scene on a frozen and white-edged canal?

For a time canal and road keep their distance but the latter soon turns sharp left and then right. Just east of the second bend, canal and railway went their separate ways with the railway opting for a more southerly route leaving the road sandwiched between the two. Just before the bend there was a stone arch bridge which replaced an earlier swivel bridge; no trace of either remains. However, a milestone has survived in situ, though minus its 5½-mile plate, to the east of the bridge crossing and beside the fence to a stable paddock. The line of the canal to the west is virtually non-existent as it has been ploughed into the lower roadside edge of the field . . . even with the strong stone evidence of the embankment wall which flanks the northern edge of the road, the imagination has to work hard to see the line of the canal above. Shortly before

the road swings south again, the overgrown canal embankment is more clearly defined as it heads off north-east to disappear under a modern bungalow, appropriately named Aqua Way.

7   Turn right onto the A367 (Fosse Way) and 100 yards on, opposite the bus-stop, turn sharp right off it and up the lane (the Old Fosse Way) between the houses; at the top turn left along the lane between the row of cottages and the canal bed.

It is curious how almost any indentation in the earth's surface attracts rubbish; canals, even those in water, seem particularly vulnerable to the scattering habits of the refuse-ridden humanoid. And so it was here along what was partly Dunkerton's eastern wharf ... until, that is, the tidying instinct took over and what was once an eyesore now boasts a mantle of green complete with small pond. In the undergrowth along the northern edge a milestone (6-miles) remains in situ. By contrast, no trace remains of the bridge that, at the south-eastern end, once carried the Old Fosse Way over the canal.

C DUNKERTON'S WHARVES extended either side of the Bath to Radstock turnpike road, the Fosse Way bridge. The Camerton to Dunkerton section of the canal was the first in water; on Monday, October 1st 1798 five coal-laden boats from Camerton Colliery tested the 'road' to Dunkerton from where two loads were taken on to Bath along the turnpike road. The wharves were not completed until November and by the following Spring the Gloucester Journal was able to report that the citizens of Bath were already feeling '. . . the benefit of the Coal Canal, which is enabled to render the coal at Dunkerton Wharf, within less than four miles from hence, on a good turnpike road, at only 2s. per ton freight and tonnage; thus is a waggon or cart capable of going twice a day to Dunkerton wharf, with more ease to the horses than once to the coalworks from this place'. In May the line west from Dunkerton had been extended to Radstock and by November as far as the canal's terminal basins near Paulton. Until the problems around Combe Hay were solved, Dunkerton's Wharf and the turnpike road thus became the main outlet for the northern collieries; when Camerton New Pit opened around 1800 the pressure on Dunkerton naturally increased and probably emphasised the need for additional wharfage both sides of the road.

8 Cross the A367 to the lay-by opposite to view the canal bridge and Dunkerton Aqueduct; turn south, keeping to the main road's western footpath, and take the first road to the right.

The eastern entrance to the Fosse Way bridge was filled in when the road was widened but the deck of the original bridge and its western parapet remain as a lay-by, the road-side curb of which is the bridge's eastern parapet. Below the bridge lie the remains of the original wharf which extended west towards the aqueduct, the best view of which is from a little way up the road. The adjacent cottage, Edelweiss Farm, was probably built around 1840 as a wharfinger's house; the slip-road between the turnpike and the wharf and cottage also remains.

D DUNKERTON AQUEDUCT carried the canal over the deep and narrow Severcombe Valley; to find a suitable crossing point, the canal swept north to form an uncharacteristic wave-like loop. Today the aqueduct's southern façade is all but obscured from the road; its stone parapets, gradually succumbing to the ever-encroaching ivy, are yet another example of how the abandoned works of man so readily surrender to nature. But all is not lost, for a short walk up the road will be rewarded by a good view of the northern face.

E Dunkerton's original SWAN INN, cleverly disguised as today's Swan Villa, is about 100 yards downhill on the left. The building pre-dates the canal so became associated with it rather by default; many other pubs and ale-houses that owed their existence to the canal (and usually faced it) have, like the waterway on their doorstep, disappeared. William 'Strata' Smith often stayed here while supervising construction work on the canal and here too, in 1832, the unpopular Rev Skinner met up with a bit of bother: 'Just as I came to the Swan Inn my carriage was recognised, on account of the grey horse which drew it, and I was assailed by about 50 Brutes, who stood outside the Ale House, clapping their hands and using the most abusive words.'

Heading west again, the line of the railway on the right is soon joined by the canal embankment before the latter swings off to the north in search of another aqueduct and another walk.

9 Turn left by Dunkerton Church, cross the Cam Brook and turn left again through the kissing-gate to follow the path alongside the Brook.

In such a gentle setting it seems almost inappropriate to mention that the Rector of Dunkerton between 1820 and 1855, Rev C F Bampfylde, was also known as as the 'Devil of Dunkerton'. It appears that his colleague at Camerton, Rev Skinner, had little time for him: 'No very inviting weather for a walk; however, I took one for the sake of exercise, with Joseph, and made a circuit along the canal to Dunkerton. I saw a large party skaiting and supposed they were some of Mr Bampfylde's acquaintances or connections. I am rather surprised that this unprincipled fellow can have anyone of the grade of gentleman at his table; but this is among the fearful tokens of the times . . . Were I called upon for my opinion of the said Mr Bampfylde, I should say I do not believe there is a more worthless fellow in the West of England.'

10 Continue on the south side of the Cam Brook to the A367; climb the steps onto the road, cross it and turn left to rejoin the river-side path via another flight of steps.

F The busy A367 was originally a so-called TURNPIKE ROAD — a Turnpike Trust milepost, dated 1827, stands on the kerbside here on the border between the parishes of Dunkerton and Wellow. The earliest turnpikes (gates where travellers paid tolls to help maintain the roads) date from 1663 when Parliament authorised the first three such gates on the Great North Road. In 1703 the first Turnpike Trust was established whereby a road (in Northamptonshire) was placed under the control of a group of trustees. The idea caught on slowly at first but between 1751 and 1772 the turnpikes had their 'manic' period when some 389 new 'trusts' were set up; an improvement in road engineering in the late 1820s saw a further boom.

11 Continue to follow the Cam-side path to the Combe Hay-Wellow road; it crosses several stiles and some plank-bridges but rarely leaves the side of the Brook.

Though seldom this close, the gurgling waters of the tiny Cam are a constant and friendly companion to the walker between Midford and Paulton. The Brook has, of course, tumbled through this gentle valley since time immemorial, long before man began exploiting its natural resources, both geographical and geological. Just as the fold of the Cam valley was the topographical basis for the SCC's Dunkerton line, the Radstock line followed the Wellow Brook and together as the Midford Brook they accompanied the canal to the Avon.

12 Cross the Combe Hay-Wellow road via the gates and continue to follow the Cam until it swings to the right; continue straight up the hill towards the driveway to Combe Hay Manor, cross the stile and turn right onto the main road.

13 Keep left and downhill where the road forks, remaining on this road for the short walk back to the *Wheatsheaf*.

SHOPS: None . . . so stock with your favourite goodies before setting off!

SUSTENANCE: The *Wheatsheaf* (Courage) at Combe Hay provides sole succour to the weak and weary, the thirsty and hungry . . . and excellent it is too!

Combe Hay Aqueduct and the railway embankment

37

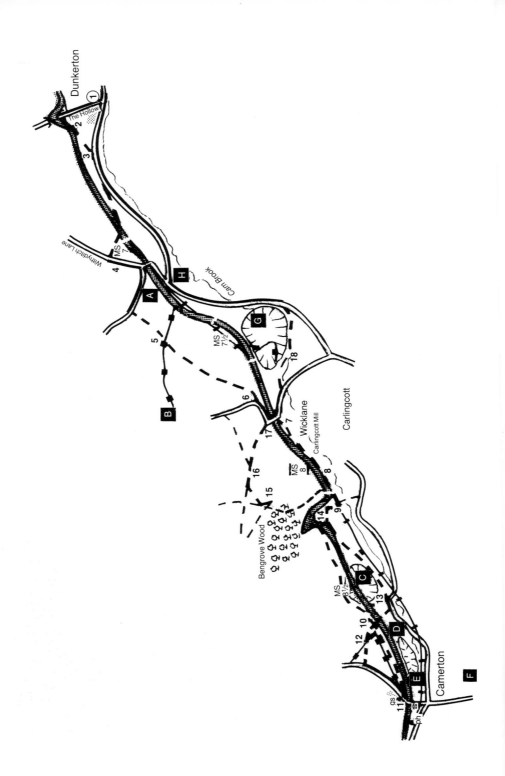

Walk 4 : Dunkerton to Camerton.

Start Point: ST 71065935. 6 miles.

This walk is the first to penetrate the north Somerset coalfield where the collieries not only outlived the canal but also left more monumental remains in the shape of overgrown spoil heaps or batches. These survive today as bizarre memorials to those who lived and died for coal.

Access: The best parking is on the road alongside Dunkerton church. Several Badgerline services, mostly to and from Bath, pass along the nearby A367; there is an infrequent and very long direct connection to Bristol – details from Bath (0225) 464446 or Bristol (0272) 553231.

Before breakfast I sent my servant, Heal, to see whether the coal barge I had ordered to be prepared to convey the ladies to Combe Hay was ready. All being arranged according to my orders, the party arrived about ten o'clock and went almost immediately to the canal. To screen them from the sun there was an awning carried over the centre of the vessel and a table and chairs placed beneath. As all Mr Boodle's children and two nurses, with the man-servant, were of the party from Radstock we mustered fifteen on board. My horse, under the direction of a man from the coal works, towed us along. We first visited the head of the canal at Paulton basin, and returned thence through Camerton and Dunkerton to Combe Hay. Having explored the beautiful grounds, etc, we partook of our cold collation under the shade of the elm trees near the cascade, and in the cool of the evening proceeded homewards. Passing the 'Swan' at Dunkerton, the Camerton band came on board and played marches and Scotch airs the whole way home. The music and the dressed-out coal barge attracted multitudes, who followed our course along the banks of the canal and lined the bridges under which we passed, which gave a novel appearance to the scenery and a pleasing termination to our rural fête.
(Journal of a Somerset Rector: John Skinner, entry for June 5th 1822)

Camerton New Pit's batch

1 Leave the main road and turn north up The Hollow; after 150 yards turn left up a few steps and follow the path to the kissing-gate at the top.

A little further up The Hollow, just beyond the cottages on the left, there was once a short aqueduct which took the canal across the road; there are no visible remains save the canal's northern boundary fences. At the top of the lane, to the right of the kissing-gate, the canal crossed under a small bridge, Coates, which carried the lane on to Manor Farm.

2 Turn left and after about 40 yards turn right and cross the recently-constructed stile into the field and continue onto the raised part of the field – the remains of the canal/railway.

This stile replaces a barbed wire fence made accessible via strategically-placed stepping stones ... an age-old 'right-of-way problem' that occurs here in reverse for, though there are several designated paths between road and canal bed, locals use the line of the canal/railway as their dog-walking 'right-of-way'.

3 Cross the field diagonally left and join the road via the gate, turn right and rejoin the field by the next gate, crossing it diagonally left towards the well-hidden stile by the gate under the embankment; cross the field heading for the buildings on Withyditch Lane.

The railway bed is fairly well defined, less so the canal where it swings north and away from the railway to follow the contour towards Withyditch Lane and the Baptist Church. In the south-west corner of the field a brick railway bridge, its arch infilled, carries Withyditch Lane towards Carlingcott; this replaced an earlier, squatter, span over the canal.

4 Cross into Withyditch Lane, turn left, then right just before the bridge; just beyond the stone cottage on the left enter the field via the kissing-gate, cross it and keep alongside its left-hand edge.

Derelict canal-side buildings near Dunkerton

A DUNKERTON PUMPING STATION stood on the south bank of the canal some 60 yards west of the bridge. The pump lifted water from the Cam 100 yards below . . . from the mill-pond where its waters were already accustomed to gather in the service of Dunkerton Mill which the SCC bought in 1802. During the 1840s the pump at Combe Hay (see Walk 2) was dismantled and brought here where it continued in service until the canal closed. In 1887, with trade on the canal increasingly suffering from railway competition, the SCC had to find additional money to purchase a new boiler for Dunkerton. Another problem arose in 1890 when the Timsbury Coal Company, suppliers of coal on preferential terms, threatened to discontinue supplies unless the SCC made a substantial payment on account. Without water the canal could not even begin to compete with the railway so the account was probably hastily settled, possibly from the revenue received at this time from the sale of old iron tramway rails. When the SCC did close on November 11th 1898, it was the cessation of pumping here that sealed the canal's fate and made the passage of boats impossible. In 1907 the GWR sold the site and its buildings to Dunkerton Collieries Ltd who, as evidenced by the scattered brick remains that mark the site, almost immediately razed the whole lot to the ground.

5 Cross into the next field via the kissing-gate and continue straight across to the three-barred stile. The next field has been sewn, so turn left and follow its edge all the way round to the gate on the other side.

From the hillside vantage point the line of the canal/railway remains visible in the valley below – and yes, the water down there *is* a small length of canal though it survives cleverly disguised as a pond! At a bend in the canal to the west there was once a broad basin, the site of a tramway wharf.

B HILL'S COLLIERY was sited 500 yards to the north-west of the canal and linked to it via a tramway and an inclined plane. The tramway was known locally as 'Dunkerton New Railway' and the pit, abandoned through flooding in the 1820s, also claimed the 'Dunkerton' label. However, some local historians have thrown doubt on whether or not the tramroad was ever built as, at the time of writing, no remains have yet been found. As what is normally referred to as Dunkerton Colliery began life as such in 1905, the 'Dunkerton Colliery' mentioned by Sydney Bourne in his account of trade to Seend in Wiltshire in the 1890s (see Walk 1) is likely to have been Camerton New Colliery.

The overgrown batch of Dunkerton Colliery (see below) dominates the valley to the south. Alongside its northern edge the canal embankment remains fairly intact and here too are the ruins of some canalside buildings built between 1812 and 1840. One of these was probably originally a canalside ale-house and after the canal's closure continued as such serving a new clientele, the miners from Dunkerton Colliery. Beneath the batch lie the remains of a tramroad that linked the canal with a limestone quarry 300 yards to the south-west.

6 Leave the field via the gate, turn left onto the road and follow it round to the left and over the brick railway bridge; turn right off the road just beyond the bridge, over the stile.

The brick road bridge clearly has its origins in the Railway Age but, as elsewhere, it marks the site of an earlier stone bridge over the canal. Just beyond the bridge was Dunkerton Colliery Halt which fell into disuse with the closure of Dunkerton Colliery in 1925.

7 Follow the narrow path down to the stile and cross into the field; turn right and follow its edge round to the next stile and cross this to climb onto the line of the railway.

The path joins the line of the railway where it crosses that of the canal but they soon sort themselves out and the railway path continues west alongside and below the canal embankment. The slope of the embankment is climbable and the towpath and bed above are both well preserved ... one of those almost secret places where a little water and a few boats are easily recreated in the mind's eye. The view south is of interest too, for down in the valley is Carlingcott Mill, its wheel once turned by the diverted waters of the adjacent Cam, its miller, according to Rev Skinner, once up to no good. 'There was a wedding by license this morning, the miller of Cridlingcot and a woman from Wellow. This was to be kept very secret, and I perceived the reason, for the bride was already far advanced in the way which women sometimes are who love their lords. This frequently occurs amongst the lower class of society, but I did not think those who moved a step higher adopted the fashion.'

8 Remain on the railway bed as far as the next stile on the left; cross this and turn right into the field to follow the path down and round to the stile at the bottom of the field.

9 Turn right onto the metalled track, cross the cattle grid and follow the track as it turns left round the corner of a house; at the next house turn right off the track to follow the path up the slope, crossing a stile and following the fence as it skirts the northern edge of the batch.

Looking north from the cattle grid, the line of the canal forms a horseshoe bend round three sides of the hill ahead. At the north-west corner of the bend (the eastern side is featured as part of the walk back to Dunkerton) a stream fed into the canal and the canal widened to form a small receptive lake – in winter a popular skating rink for, among others, the Rev Skinner and his family: '... the boys took their gun and their skaites immediately after our breakfast and went to the basin at Bengrove, but as snow had fallen in the night were obliged to employ sweepers'.

C CAMERTON NEW PIT's spoil heap gradually rose skywards between the early 19th century and 1950. Underground, the pit was linked to

Camerton Old Pit and both were initially managed by the lord of the manor, James Stephens. Here, in 1893, there was an explosion caused by coal dust igniting during shot-firing, the first, but not the last, such incident in the Somerset coalfield. In his diary John Skinner frequently refers to incidents at the Camerton collieries such as the extraordinary death of Aaron Horler in July 1803. 'He had been drinking at the public house, whence, after behaving in a violent manner by dancing on the tables and stools, etc, and insulting some of his associates there assembled, he walked to the Lower Pit and, it is supposed, endeavoured to slide down the rope (by which the coal is hauled) to the bottom; but going too quick, not being able to retain his hold, he fell down many fathoms and was dashed to pieces, his hands being much burnt by the velocity with which the rope passed through them before he let go his hold. A person going down to the pit about ten o'clock to feed the asses kept under-ground was presented with this horrid spectacle on his descent, and was so much frightened as not to recover himself for some time.' A century on and the canal had gone but New Pit continued to work, its spoil heap gradually spilling over atop the bed of the redundant waterway while its southern face embraced a railway siding.

10 Leave the field alongside the batch via the kissing-gate, continue across the open space and straight on along the track towards Camerton.

D NEW PIT WHARF was one of the SCC's main coal wharves; the pit was right beside the canal, just south of the 'open space' referred to above, and was linked to Old Pit via a narrow-gauge tramway (the track down to Camerton). It was probably to and from this wharf that one of the last traders to use the canal, Adam Wragg of Seend, worked his narrow boats Phoebe, Anne and Queen. A fire under the pit boiler and the subsequent re-siting of this, the winding gear and generator caused the in-filling of part of the wharf in 1904–5; by the time the pit closed in 1950 virtually all traces of the canal and its wharf had gone . . . a path the colliery buildings were themselves soon to follow. In addition to the tramroad from Old Pit, another linked the colliery with Meadgate Coal Depot to the north and crossed over the canal at the end of the wharf.

The walk to Camerton runs parallel to the canal along the line of the Old Pit-New Pit tramroad, the track of which was lifted in 1910. For most of its length the canal ditch, nestling in the shadow of Old Pit's long and low wooded batch, is not only visible but looks good enough to be in water! At the track's eastern end the red-brick building marks the line of a similar narrow-gauge tramroad to Meadgate while, opposite, New Pit's erstwhile canteen has become a bungalow. On the right, at the Camerton end, stands a church room erected in memory of Emily Elizabeth Jarrett who died in 1911. Round to the right and over a stile a battery of boards interprets pits, canal and railway ... all of which is overseen by a large, fibre-glass 'jolly collier' (a replica of a bronze statue created for the National Coal Board's contribution to the 1951 Festival of Britain) that, until recently, adorned the car park of the *Jolly Collier* (see page 48).

11 At the road turn left initially and cross the stile to view the site of Old Pit, Camerton Wharf and the 'Jolly Collier's' new home before continuing uphill to the 'park bench' on the right by the stile; cross this and head diagonally left for the stile opposite.

E A concrete-capped shaft of CAMERTON OLD PIT lies unassumingly amid a derelict patch of green edged by a busy road . . . the unmarked grave of a way of life that began here in the 1780s. The road went right through the colliery while the canal passed under the road just south of the capped shaft. There was a canal basin too here with a wharf to the south; the basin was hemmed in by two bridges, one a small wooden structure that carried the tramway from New Pit and the other a stone road bridge to the west. It was from here that the first coal-laden boats (see Walk 3) were loaded for that inaugural trip to Dunkerton on October 1st 1798 . . . ironically both the canal and the pit

closed exactly a century later. In his inimitable style John Skinner recalls an incident at the pit in March 1806: 'James Edwards, whose business it was to see the coal brought to land at The Old Pit, in reaching over too far in order to stay the basket which was coming up, fell to the bottom and was dashed to pieces. Horrid to say, his last word was an oath when he found himself going. He left a widow and four children at Cridlingcot.' Never short of a word, Rev Skinner involved himself as a sort of unofficial arbitrator during a period of unrest at the Camerton pits in December 1830: 'I saw all was quiet on the Down, and the Steam Engine working, as I approach the pit. I walked thither, and found that the Radstock Rioters, for I can call them by no other name, had gone on to Paulton. The people at the pit said they were well satisfied with their wages, but that these fellows from Radstock had ordered them to stop work. I counselled them against cutting the ropes of the pits and the damaging of machinery etc, and advised them to return to their duty: that there were barges then waiting for their loads. The men said they would load the barges, and should not stop work; that they had nothing to complain of, only that they thought the small coal landed ought to be paid for as well as the large coal, since they procured one as well as the other.' Skinner went on to note: '. . . that there was no distress among them was sufficiently proved by the increased number of public houses; if the men were in want of food, they could not support the trade of eleven public houses, instead of three'.

12 Cross the stile and the bridge and turn right down the lane, cross the 'open space' and head on downhill to the road; turn left.

F Although neither the REV JOHN SKINNER'S church nor his rectory are part of this walk, his spirit has accompanied most of the canal's route from Dundas. As is probably evident from his oft-quoted words, Skinner was a man of strongly-held and forcefully-voiced views; he was not a popular man locally, particularly with those who worked in the pits: 'After dinner we walked to the canal, my sons wishing to sail in the boat, as the wind blew fresh; they amused themselves awhile. As Anna and myself were returning home by Colliers Row, a stone was thrown at me from the end house, where Goold lives; it could have been no other, as the stone came from that direction. There is really not a day passes over my head but I meet with some fresh insult.' That was 1830, nine years before his death, an event put in all its miserable perspective by Virginia Woolf in the conclusion to her introduction to his diaries: 'There was nothing left to live for. Yet what had he done to make every one hate him? Why did the farmers call him mad? Why did Joseph [his son] say that no one would read what he wrote? Why did the villagers tie tin cans to the tail of his dog? Why did the peacocks shriek and the bells ring? Why was there no mercy shown to him and no respect and no love? With agonising repetition the diary asks these questions; but there was no answer. At last, one morning in October 1839, the Rector took his gun, walked into the beech wood near his home, and shot himself dead.' Joseph was wrong!

13 Turn left off the road where it bends to the right and follow the path, which soon crosses a stile, along the southern edge of New Pit's batch; at the eastern end of the batch follow the path across the field heading for the stile to the left of the enclosed garden.

En route to Carlingcott atop the hill, the road crosses over the Cam and between the redundant abutments of the railway, the line of which soon becomes indistinguishable from the path alongside the spoil heap. To walk in the shadow of the conifer-covered batch is to wonder at the irony of it all . . . that something that began as an eyesore, as an unsolicited blot on the landscape, should so readily cast aside its origins and gently mellow into such glorious maturity.

14 Cross the stile, turn right and follow the outward route back towards the cattle grid; turn left before this, go through the kissing-gate just beyond the house and continue up the hill towards Bengrove Wood.

Where the track crossed the canal a cottage, now called Sellar's Stile, was known locally as the 'lock-keeper's' cottage. Clearly this was an inaccurate description, though it is likely that it had some other association with the canal – probably a lengthsman's cottage. The track linked Bengrove Pit (also known as Cuckoo and Dunkerton Old Pit), 500 yards to the north, with Wicklane. Its lower length runs parallel to the canal bed – now an attractive garden – before closing in and becoming increasingly overgrown. As compensation near the top, the view across and down to Camerton New Pit's lofty batch is quite breathtaking and, in certain lights, more than a little awesome. The imagination is left to fill in the detail . . . the line of the canal where it skirts its northern edge before disappearing into it and, beyond and below, the disused line of the railway.

15 Head for the track through the wood. At the top, cross the open space between the fields and continue north, keeping the hedge on the right; cross through the kissing-gate at the top.

It is often difficult for walkers to equate the morality of farmers who cultivate rights of way with their own sense of right and wrong when it comes to crossing such fields . . . to go round the edge is not only time-consuming but can also condone the ploughing in of paths; to opt for the direct route between two stiles can damage part of a valuable crop. While offering no moral guidance, it must be said that in this case the right-hand edge of the field does look down across the Cam valley to, on the one hand, Dunkerton Colliery's batch and, on the other, the hilltop village of Carlingcott and, in the valley below, its picturesque Cam-side mill.

16 Cross the field diagonally right to a stile, cross this and the next field diagonally left to another stile; finally cross the next field diagonally left towards the gateway.

17 **Go through the gateway and turn immediately right to cross the road-bridge; continue downhill and turn left up the track just before the bridge over the Cam.**

Initially the path runs alongside a hill-side vineyard, the northern edge of which sits atop the bed of the canal/railway. Meanwhile, as ever, the Cam rattles along on the right to be joined before long by the towering presence of Dunkerton Colliery's batch opposite . . . in such a setting it is hard to believe that all of this, even the little Cam, was once part and parcel of a thriving industrial landscape.

G DUNKERTON COLLIERY'S spoil heap is a relatively new 'blot on the landscape'. The pit was opened in 1905, seven years after the canal closed, and therefore had no direct connection with it. Although it soon became the largest colliery in the area, it 'enjoyed' a particularly bad reputation, its masters seemingly having more of an eye to profit than safety . . . little wonder the miners rioted during a strike over the winter of 1908-9. After the Great War, the pit experienced financial problems and closed in 1925; proposals to re-open it, the most recent in 1946, came to nothing.

18 **The batch-side path crosses the Cam before joining the road; turn left here and remain on the road for about half a mile before turning right towards Dunkerton Church.**

The road crosses the Cam once again, the picturesque bridge adorned with a cast-iron 'weight-restriction' plate . . . though information on the weights restricted is vague to say the least! The track on the left a little further on was the entrance to Dunkerton Colliery; a brief sortie up it reveals, amongst the general mêlée, some old office buildings.

H A bend in the original course of the CAM BROOK was, in addition to several natural feeders, a major source of water for the canal. Before the canal company bought the nearby mill this was a mill pond, a natural reservoir that was easily tapped with the aid of the

canal-side Pumping Station above. All that remains is the circular pond clearly visible from the Dunkerton road just below its junction with Withyditch Lane. Following the recent diversion of the Cam to a much straighter course further south, it was decided, for conservation purposes, to save the pond from the plough.

The canal and railway embankment remain as a constant high-rise companion for the rest of the walk back to the start point by Dunkerton Church.

SHOPS: Camerton Post Office and General Store offers the only provisions en route.

SUSTENANCE: Most of the eleven ale houses are no more and, worse still, the *Jolly Collier* at Camerton is now gone. The only way to quench a raging thirst on this walk is to head half-a-mile north from Camerton to the *Camerton Inn* (Free House).

The Cam Brook and Dunkerton Colliery's batch

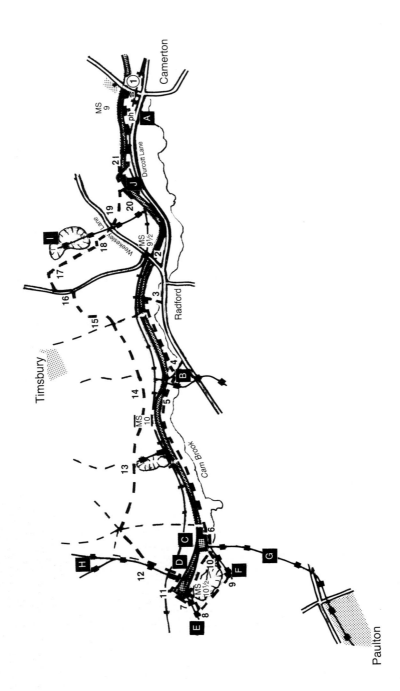

Walk 5 : Camerton to Timsbury.

Start Point: ST 68115793. 5 miles.

A walk that, perhaps more than any other, establishes the canal's *raison d'être* – the cluster of collieries that once clung to the hillsides around Timsbury and Paulton. All have now gone, the scars have healed but the evidence, overgrown and unkempt, remains.

Access: There is off-the-road parking for a few cars by the start point just west of Camerton Post Office and the resited fibre-glass Jolly Collier, the latter now redundant from overseeing patrons using the car park of the sadly missed local that bore his name. An infrequent (ex Sunday) Badgerline service (667) between Bristol and Writhlington stops by the PO; details from Bristol (0272) 553231.

Whilst walking in the village, as I generally do between Morning and Evening Services in order to see things are tolerably quiet, I saw a boat laden with coal going down the Canal. On enquiring whose it was I found that it was under the direction of William Goold, junr, who carried coal for his brother, Joseph Goold. I told the boys who were with it how improper it was to be boating coal on a Sunday, and begged they would tell their master I should notice the impropriety of this behaviour. The name of the barge was 'Vulcan No. 7'. On Monday I went to Goold's, found he was with the boat, and was not expected home for a day or two. I desired they would send him to my house when he came home. Friday he came up after breakfast, said he was very sorry for what he had done, but was fearful he should not get his coal up into the country if he had not done as he did, as there was likely to be a stoppage on the canal; that he knew I might have him fined, but if I would not proceed against him he would never be guilty of the like in future.
(Journal of a Somerset Rector: John Skinner, entry for August 20th 1809).

Walking the line near Radford

1 Head south from Camerton PO and turn into the first road on the right, Durcott Lane.

It is tempting to begin this walk by following the canal towpath that runs west from the start point ... saving it till the end gives the SCC addict a last and lasting glimpse of a cut that the Rector of Camerton, John Skinner, and his entourage clearly savoured all those years ago. Were it not for new housing, the line of the canal would stand out clearly along the valley wall to the north; nevertheless from the road there are satisfying glimpses of the embankment running behind the hotch-potch of buildings either side of the former *Jolly Collier*.

A   An outcrop of new housing straddles what was once the car park of the JOLLY COLLIER, a reminder that, in its twilight years, this canalside local showed its face to the road and an increasingly mobile clientele. Back in the early 19th century, as the New or Camerton Inn of Skinner's day, its regulars were more associated with the new canal and thus, like most canalside pubs, its frontage was that way inclined. Skinner normally had little time for public houses and their patrons, however he seems to have made an exception of his own 'local'. 'Having engaged one of the coal barges, I had it fitted up for the ladies with an awning and matting against the side, and tables and chairs from the public house ...' The Camerton Inn was probably built specifically for the canal trade; as the section between Camerton and Radford was one of the first to be completed in May 1799, it may even have been the first of the SCC's many canalside ale houses ... hopefully it will be the last to become a private residence.

The railway passed under Camerton Hill to the north of Durcott Lane converging on the road close to the pub. Homes now straddle the railway embankment while the canal above and behind has, for once, escaped Planning Man's pen and, as we shall see, the remains of Lower Conygre Colliery Wharf lurk in the undergrowth up there. Where the road kinks to the left railway and canal met; the line of the latter now hugs the northern edge of the road, its indentation barely visible ... except, that is, after prolonged heavy rainfall. Shortly before the junction with Weekesley Lane the line of the canal swings north-west, appropriately enough alongside what is now a coal-yard.

2 Turn right initially at the T-junction to walk a short distance uphill to where the canal passed under the road; turn and descend the hill back past Durcott Lane keeping right to cross the Cam Brook.

Radford is little more than a cluster of cottages clinging to the remains of the canal and railway, both of which crossed under Weekesley Lane. The loftier (railway) bridge is clearly visible, less so the canal bridge which crossed just south of the railway; the best vantage point from which to view an imaginary industrial landscape is atop the railway bridge looking west. The line of the canal is all but gone but the creative eye can visualise a triangular basin bulging north-wards over what became the bed of the railway and the site of Radford Halt. The high embankment of the canal becomes increasingly clearer from the Paulton Road between the stone cottages and Radford Mill.

3 Turn right off the road towards Radford Mill and re-cross the Cam Brook; turn left at the top of the lane and join the canal towpath via the stile where Mill Lane swings round to the right.

By Radford Mill the retaining wall of the canal's embankment is clearly defined as is the canal bed's new, though scarcely fashionable, role as a meeting place for an entanglement of cars, caravans, vans, corrugated iron and brambles. Mill Lane once crossed the canal via a swing bridge though this was later replaced by a fixed stone-arch bridge which has since been demolished. The line between Radford and Paulton opened in November 1799 thus completing the canal between Dunkerton Wharf and the terminal basins; ironically it was this same section that during the late 1880s was the first to suffer from lack of maintenance and fall into disrepair ... none of which explains the still-traceable lock-like chamber that stood west of the bridge! Heading west the canal and its towpath remain almost untouched by time.

4 Cross the stile and the field beyond heading for the telegraph pole to view, to the right, the stone remains of Radford Colliery Wharf.

B The robust stone retaining wall of RADFORD COLLIERY WHARF is clearly defined on the northern edge of the field. Here too the line of the connecting tramway between the wharf and Radford Colliery (opened in the 1790s, closed around 1847) across the Cam Brook can be clearly seen. Both were built at the same time as the canal – an advert inviting tenders for the work first appeared in the Bath Chronicle *in July 1795 – and probably fell into decay around 1850 when the pit closed.*

5 Cross the track and rejoin the canal bed via the sloped path to the left of the wharf's stonework, almost immediately crossing a stile. Continue to the next stile and cross this en route to Paulton Basin.

The canal is again well-defined here and remains so to the terminal basins less than a mile away; preserved too, like a lone tombstone, is the plate-less milestone that once confirmed that Dundas Wharf was a mere 10 miles away. The tree-topped spoil heap to the north holds the earthly remnants of Withy Mills Colliery, a tramway along the eastern side of which joined the canal just west of the milestone. The tramway fed boats on the canal from 1815 until the pit's closure in the late 1870s. Nearer to Paulton Basin parts of the cut actually hold water ... though, it must be admitted, scarcely enough to satisfy even a plastic duck!

6 Turn left over the next stile and continue alongside the canal to the remains of the old dry dock. Cross the adjacent stile and continue beside Paulton Basin and onwards to Timsbury Basin.

C PAULTON BASIN is the first of two basins that together form the canal's terminus. Just before the canal widens are the scattered stone remains of a bridge; this was built to facilitate horse-drawn boats using the northern towing path to and from the wharves at Timsbury Basin. Until recently, another simple stone bridge took the southern towpath across a short arm adjoining the south-east corner of the basin; this was a dry dock which could accommodate two narrow boats. Paulton Basin looked south to the collieries clinging to the hills around the eastern purlieus of Paulton, most of which were fed by a tramway and its branches that joined the canal here at Paulton Basin. Just south and west of the basin two new aluminum bridges cross the Cam Brook on the site of their recently removed stone antecedents. Beneath their stark aluminium spans outcrops of the original stone abutments remain as a small memorial to the grit and grime of a bustling industrial landscape that has all but vanished. Both bridges were built to accommodate tramways that rattled down the hillside to the basin, the more westerly one from Paulton Lower Engine Pit and Paulton Foundry.

D The canal soon widens out into TIMSBURY BASIN, the end of the line for all boats but in particular those being served by the northern collieries. The southern waterfront, however, was far from inactive for, at its western end, the tramway from Paulton Upper Engine Pit joined the canal – once again the line is easily traced to and across a stone bridge spanning the Cam Brook to the south. Nevertheless, as the 'Timsbury' appellation suggests, it was here that the tramways from the pits scattered between High Littleton and Timsbury converged. It was here too that the buildings and paraphernalia of a thriving working waterway gathered to open up new and far-flung markets for Somerset's coal. Not surprisingly, the trade in boats was an important part of the overall picture. In 1810, for example, Mr Crang of Timsbury advertised the sale of 'four canal boats ... repaired and with cabins' which would 'carry 25 tons each'; a month later Crang was selling five such boats by auction.

A lone hawthorn tree grows out from the wharfside masonry, an unwitting witness to what is, to all intents and purposes, the end of the line; even the first and last milestone, 10½ miles from Dundas, is no more. But Paulton and Timsbury Basins, tucked away in the verdant valley of the Cam Brook, are neither beginnings nor ends but rather integral parts of a story that begins in the pits of North Somerset. Before leaving this valley, therefore, a short foray along the remains of some of the connecting tramways can only serve to put the canal and its collieries into their industrial context.

7 Turn south-west from Timsbury Basin to cross the stile and the bridge over the Cam Brook; continue up the hillside via the enclosed path.

The tramway that linked the collieries with the SCC were almost as much part of the canal as the boats that carried the coal down to the K&A and beyond. More often than not gravity was the cheap and cheerful motive force behind the coal-laden waggons but, where gravity was clearly pointing the wrong way, man and/or beast assumed the responsibility of keeping the waggons rolling. Here the tramway down from Paulton Upper Engine Pit is clearly defined as is the adjacent batch; however, the pit itself is cleverly disguised as a sewage farm.

8 Turn left onto the tarmaced road by the sewage farm and follow the path that runs south-east from the gate.

E Dating from the 1750s, PAULTON UPPER & LOWER ENGINE PITS, the oldest in this part of the coalfield, were so-called because they boasted a steam engine (a Newcomen atmospheric) to help overcome the perennial problem of inadequate drainage. Another claim to fame was the tragedy that occurred on March 24th 1830 when four men and a boy ascending the shaft were killed. Rev Skinner's diary for March 30th recalls the event in all its stark simplicity. 'We walked to Paulton after dinner, and attended the funerals of five of the colliers who were killed by the breaking

of the rope last week; two more are expected to die.' Normally men were brought up and down in loops attached to the winding rope that lowered and raised the coal hudge, a large iron barrel. On this occasion the thick hemp rope broke and nine persons fell 50ft to the bottom of the shaft, quickly followed by 600ft of heavy rope. In 1861 the SCC and Paulton Engine Coal Co were in dispute and, despite the proximity of the pits to the canal, the trade was lost to the Radstock & Frome Railway. The pits closed around 1870.

9 Bear left at the site of Paulton Foundry (just after the stone stile) and continue downhill back to Paulton Basin.

F PAULTON FOUNDRY was established in 1810 and served the collieries and the local domestic market with their needs until the 1890s . . . everything from winding and pumping engines for the pits to cast-iron gateposts, some of which can still be found along the lanes of North Somerset. The cast iron accommodation bridge that used to span the canal near Monkton Combe (see Walk 1) once bore two plates that read CAST AT PAULTON 1811.

From the site of William Evans' Paulton Foundry, the track down to and across the Cam Brook (via the new girder bridge) follows the line of the tramway to Paulton Basin. This same tramway served both the foundry and Paulton Lower Engine Pit and thus saw a more diverse traffic; one such trade seems to have been in the sandstone blocks brought in by the foundry from Temple Cloud for transhipment, possibly by canal, for use on the Radstock tramway.

10 Cross the Cam and turn left to rejoin the towpath back (see 6 above) to the head of navigation at Timsbury Basin.

G The main SOUTHERN TRAMWAY, east of the tramway from Paulton Lower Engine Pit, linked the canal at Paulton Basin with several collieries, the first of which, Brittens Lower, was sited at the tramway's junction with the Paulton

Road. In its 1.4 miles the tramway was fed by some five other pits; Paulton Ham (ST 65555640), Paulton Hill (ST 65545620), Simons Hill (ST 65875616), Salisbury Lower (ST 65925580) and possibly Salisbury Middle (ST 65685574). By 1850 only Brittens and the Salisbury pits were still active; use of the tramway was discontinued in the 1870s.

11 Turn right at the end of Timsbury Basin and head north-east towards the well-defined gap (bridge abutments that once carried the C&LSR) in the northern perimeter of the field; follow the line of the tramway across the lower end of the next field towards the stile and gate.

The stile referred to above is not only a good place at which to take a breather before the climb back to Camerton but also offers good views back to the canal and its basins. Looking north there is little to see but a lot to imagine for it was here that the two branches of the northern tramway converged.

H Via its two branches the NORTHERN TRAMWAY linked the canal with the collieries to the north and north-west. The Timsbury branch came in from the north and was fed by five pits: Grove (ST 66015834), Old Grove (ST 65885842), New Grove (ST 66025860), New Tyning (ST 65885870) and Hayeswood (ST 65825911); the Mearns branch, which was originally to have been extended to take in the Clutton collieries, came in from the north-west and was fed by two pits; Mearns (ST 65215876) and Amesbury (ST 65495869). Amesbury dates from about 1701 but it was abandoned because of flooding during the early 1800s. Hayeswood also suffered from flooding problems and in February 1845 seven men and four boys working at the coal face were drowned by a sudden surge of water from old workings; the pit was closed but re-opened in 1856 and finally shut down six years later.

12 Enter the next field and cross diagonally right towards the stile

Minus its plate, the 10-mile milestone near Radford

midway along its eastern perimeter; cross this, turn right onto the lane and immediately bear left at the entrance to the farm.

The lane offers excellent views down across the valley to Paulton and Timsbury Basins and various connected landmarks on the southern valley wall. It is a generally green and agricultural landscape that belies its industrial origins but nevertheless one that the imaginary eye can easily piece together. But there is a stillness here too and though the sights of the industrial past can be recreated, the sounds and smells that must have hovered over this valley are ever-elusive. Suddenly the overgrown batch of Withy Mills Colliery (opened 1815, closed by 1877) dominates the view south while the scar of one of its disused shafts is clearly visible in the field opposite.

13 Keep right at the entrance up to the next farm and cross the stile to follow the track down towards the canal and along the back of Dunford Farm.

14 Take the track uphill at the fork east of Dunford Farm; at the top bear left through the gate and down across the track (Mill Lane) via the gap between two trees and the stile opposite.

The views down to and across the valley continue to be impressive with both canal and railway vieing for attention; Radford Mill is down there too . . . no prizes therefore for working out the destination of Mill Lane!

15 Follow the path down and round to the left to where it crosses the stream via a small wooden bridge; cross this and continue uphill to the stile in the far corner of the field.

16 Cross the stile and another a few yards further on and continue uphill to a third stile; cross onto the road (Radford Hill) and turn left.

At the top of Radford Hill is the village of Timsbury, its mining tradition little more than a memory recorded in a few street names. Not surprisingly Timsbury once boasted several hostelries, relaxing retreats for miners eager to wash the coal dust out of their throats; only two remain, the *Seven Stars* and the *Guss and Crook*. As its sign graphically illustrates, the latter took its name from the harness used by the colliery lads to haul the laden sledges to the base of the shaft – the *guss* was the waistband of leather or rope from which a chain was attached to the sledge by a hook . . . or by *crook*.

17 At the brow of the hill turn right off the road up the track; at the stile 'crossroads' turn right down into the field, keep to the left-hand perimeter and cross the stile at the southern end of Lower Conygre Pit's spoil heap.

18 Cross the culverted stream and continue uphill before turning left under the old railway incline and into the field; keeping the wood close by on the left, cut across the field to the gate onto the road.

I LOWER CONYGRE PIT opened in 1858 and the following year was linked by tramway to the canal below. By 1900 it had moved into the Railway Age and was linked to the S&D main line near Radford Halt by an incline. Further attempts at modernisation followed and much was spent on exploration that gave little or no return. The much older Upper Conygre Pit (opened in 1791) was sited some distance away on the northern outskirts of Timsbury. Though there was no tramway link to the canal, some coal was sent by road to Conygre Wharf near Camerton and there was also an underground link between the two pits. Both closed in 1916 when the coal faces encountered a major geological fault and the Lower Pit was flooded from the old Withy Mills workings.

Like its various look-a-likes, Lower Conygre's batch has been embraced by nature and transformed by time into a wooded knoll that, to the casual observer, belies its man-made origins. This particular tip has been adopted by the adder and even boasts a sign warning the unwary of the fact. Nature has also been aided and abetted by Farming Man in the virtual obliteration of even the line of the tramway from Lower Conygre Pit down to the canalside wharf ... hardly surprising, perhaps, as the track was lifted in 1906! There are, however, clues to its line on opposite sides of the field in question but scarcely anything to link the two!

19 Cross the road, bearing slightly left, and enter the field opposite via the stile; cross the field diagonally left to the left-hand end of the car-repair yard (the roofs of various vehicles are visible down the hill).

20 Before crossing the stile, turn right and continue westwards along the bottom edge of the field as far as its closest point to the road; return to the stile, cross it and turn left almost immediately.

J LOWER CONYGRE WHARF lies hidden, but not lost, between the car-repair yard (atop the line of the canal) and Durcott Lane. From the edge of the field the straining neck can glimpse beyond the wharf's retaining wall and into the dark depths of the canal bed. And though there is much to see – the retaining wall itself, tramway sleeper blocks and even some coal debris – there is much to feel too in this overgrown time-trap.

21 Stay on the path that keeps on the southern edge of the canal and clearly leads to a garden gate; enter the garden, keep to the well-defined path by the house and leave the garden via a second gate opposite and remain on the towpath back to the road by Camerton PO.

Where field and path join at the eastern end of the repair yard there was once a stone hump-backed bridge; some evidence remains but it is not until reaching the Camerton side of the garden (see above) that both canal and towpath are again clearly defined. The owners of the property which the public footpath bisects are a rare breed indeed in that, having realized that their garden straddles a small piece of history, they have not sought to discourage the inquisitive stranger! For

the last lap back to the start point at Camerton the canal bed, despite its agricultural usage, is clearly defined. The front of the erstwhile *Camerton Inn*-cum-*Jolly Collier* is a bonus and helps re-create a lasting picture of what it was like on this working waterway during the 19th century ... an image given characteristically blunt substance by Rev Skinner's diary for 1803 which records that 'Another stranger ... named Culling Macnab, who also worked in the coal pits, being much intoxicated on Saturday night was drowned by falling into the Canal ... '

SHOPS: There is only the one on the walk itself - Camerton PO - though a short detour at Paulton and Timsbury opens up wider markets.

SUSTENANCE: The *Jolly Collier* at Camerton is no more. The *Guss and Crook* on the southern outskirts of Timsbury (see map) is worth the diversion northwards from either Mill Lane or Radford Hill if only to have a look at its pub-sign and confirm its compatibility with the description above! Just southwest of Radford, the *Old Malt House Hotel* serves morning coffee and afternoon teas.

A jolly collier?

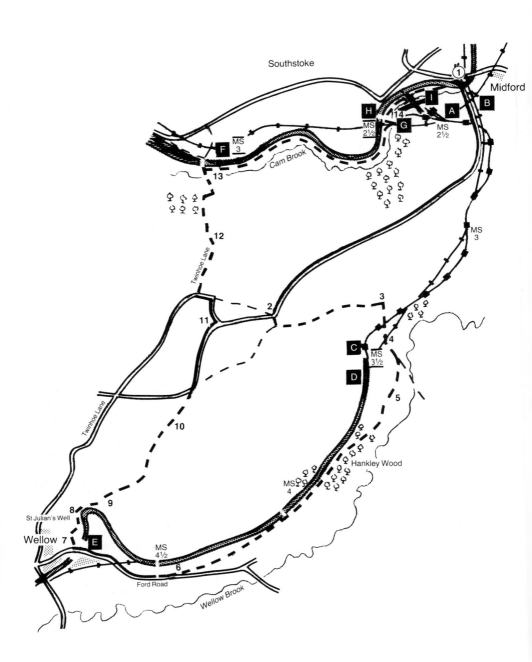

Walk 6 : Midford to Wellow.

Start Point: ST 76076063. 6½ miles.

The lack of access to the line of the canal and tramway between Midford and Wellow is compensated for by the area's natural attributes. At Wellow itself the tunnel is elusive but there is a surprise in store just around the bend . . . added to which the delights of the Dunkerton line are a bonus.

Access: Parking on main-road Midford is not advised - the road signposted to Twinhoe offers safer possibilities. On the other hand patrons of the *Hope and Anchor* may use its car-park but should seek out the landlord and let him know. Besides the obvious attraction, the pub is a good starting point for, as we have seen (Walk 1), its fireside window looks out onto the northern face of the canal bridge. Midford is on Badgerline's infrequent Frome-Bath-Bristol Swiftlink service (X3); details from Bath (0225) 464446 or Bristol (0272) 553231.

TO BE SOLD BY AUCTION
(By order of the Assignees of JOHN MAGGS, a Bankrupt)
Four substantial COAL-BOATS, three of which have been used a short time on the Kennet and Avon and Wilts and Berks CANAL, and the other which lies on the Radstock Coal Canal, is nearly new, and was sometime since moved to that line of the Canal, at a very considerable expense. The Boats are each about 25 tons burthen.
(Bath Journal, July 15th 1811)

1 Turn South off the main road, towards Twinhoe.

The bed of the canal's main line is visible from both sides of the road bridge though only as a decorative part of a long ornamental garden. Looming larger above and to the east is the Somerset & Dorset Joint Railway viaduct before the lower Camerton & Limpley Stoke version crosses over the road but under the S&D viaduct. And getting in on the action the Cam Brook weaves its time-worn course towards its confluence with the Wellow Brook . . . and a change of name for both.

The sole surviving plate-less milestone

A   The mile-long TRAMWAY between Midford Basin and Twinhoe Basin began life in 1804 as a temporary means of establishing a through route from the Radstock collieries to the Dunkerton line at Midford while money was raised to complete a flight of 19 locks. The tramway actually followed what would have been the line of the lock flight but the Canal Company's financial difficulties led to their abandonment (despite the fact that tenders for the work were sought in

The horseshoe bend at Wellow

September 1802) and, inevitably, the 'temporary' became permanent.

B It was the sale of the Radstock Tramway to the SOMERSET & DORSET RAILWAY in 1871 that was effectively the beginning of the end of the SCC. The 8-arched brick and stone viaduct here at Midford was clearly one of the railway's major engineering works and one that, as reported by the Bath Chronicle in August 1872, was soon far advanced:

> The large viaduct over the ponds at Midford is in a very forward state, both abutments and two piers being ready for the arches and three quarters of the remaining piers are completed.

When the railway opened in July 1874 it linked Radstock and its hinterland of coalfields with the Midland Railway at Bath and in doing so, emphasised all the more the deficiencies of its northern rival, the Dunkerton line of the canal.

Sadly the road deviates away from the line of the tramway and even where the two cross, the line of the railway steals the show. But there are compensations. As the road climbs away from Midford there are views east that take in the line of Wellow Brook while over to the north-west the gentle curves of the Dunkerton line of the canal and beyond it the C&LSR embankment are clearly defined along the northern slopes of the Cam valley.

2 At Middle Twinhoe turn left towards Middle Twinhoe Barns and, where the track bends round to the right, keep to the left of the stone barn to cross the stile and head across the field to the stile in the bottom left-hand corner; cross this and keep left round the field to cross the next stile and continue down the ditch-like track to the right.

3 At the bottom of the track turn right and head downhill towards the railway viaduct and embankment.

As the path descends towards Lower Twinhoe the view to the right (south) takes in Twinhoe Basin and what was originally the junction of the canal from Radstock and the tramway to and from Midford. That said there are better views to come from the railway embankment next to the viaduct under which the path passes. Looking south-west from here there are three lone tree stumps in the field and to their left a wooded clump wherein a milestone lurks at the northern end of what was Twinhoe Basin.

C TWINHOE BASIN was, for about a decade, the canal terminus of the line from Radstock. There is little documentary evidence that the canal section ever generated much traffic; with three time-consuming transhipment points – Radstock, Twinhoe and Midford – collieries might just as well have used the roads. John Maggs clearly did trade with his 25-ton coal barge as far as Twinhoe for five years up until 1811 so it is safe to assume that there were others doing the same. However, it soon became abundantly clear that the canal/tramway arrangement was unworkable and in 1814 the Canal Company decided to accept the recommendation of John Hodgkinson and extend the tramway from Twinhoe to Radstock atop the canal towpath. It seems that the single-track tramway (there were passing loops about every 600 yards) had an unusual gauge of 3ft 5½in which was probably also the gauge of the colliery tramways around Radstock as well as the Twinhoe-Midford line. Motive power was provided by teams of three horses which could haul eight or nine 27cwt waggons at 2d per ton per mile exclusive of tolls.

D As on other canals, MILESTONES on the SCC were a statutory requirement as the basis for calculating tolls. Styles and materials varied from one canal to another while some, like road-side milestones, gave distances to and from two locations. Occasionally, as was the case on the SCC and the Lancaster Canal, the same canal boasted two distinct styles of milestones – probably because the work was done by different contractors. Here on the Radstock line there were 15 milestones, solid stone slabs with a circular inset plate which indicated *distances at ½-mile intervals to the K&A at Dundas. Only the one here at Twinhoe Basin remains in situ, its missing plate having once read simply '3½'.*

The wooded clump already mentioned is all there is to see of Twinhoe Basin . . . powerful binoculars might pick out the stunted form of the milestone just within the arrow-head of trees. But no artificial aids are needed to follow the line of the tramway as it cuts purposefully across the slope of the hill west of and parallel to the railway embankment.

4 Pass under the railway viaduct, turn right and follow that path round the right-hand edge of the field; turn right at the opening into the next field, keeping to the track.

Down in the valley the chattering waters of Wellow Brook put in a more impressive appearance, if only because, as evidenced by the war-time pill-boxes, they were clearly worth defending from the enemy. Over to the west the railway and canal have become almost as one and their clearly-defined embankment is to be a constant companion for most of the way to Wellow. A glance back confirms the parting of the ways, the railway opting for a more direct easterly route, the tramway curving round the side of the hill.

5 Continue through the next gate, following the blue bridle-way signs through Hankley Wood, and through another gate into a field.

Hankley Wood soon closes in on both path and canal/railway embankment though the line of the latter is sometimes obscured by the screen of trees. This wood has been witness to a strange sequence of events starting back at the beginning of the 19th century when 'navvies' first cut a broad swathe through the valley. The water-filled cut, its stillness only occasionally interrupted by passing boats, soon gave way to the rattle of horse-drawn waggons and, after a brief transition, the inevitable surge of steam. By the spring of 1966 all was quiet again and

nature began the slow process of reclaiming the privacy of this bosky vale.

6 Keep to the path along the left-hand perimeter of the field and eventually join Ford Road via the gate and sloped path; turn right towards Wellow.

The gap in the fence of the field just beyond Hankley Wood marks the site of what used to be known as Gibb's Fixed Bridge; this was demolished before 1840, long before the line of the railway wreaked further havoc. But the canal has survived in places and a little further to the south-west, where the railway takes a slightly straighter line, the towpath embankment can still be made out.

7 Continue along the road into Wellow and turn right off the road just before the Church; cross the stile at the end of the path and the next one dead ahead, then turn right.

The walk into Wellow is dominated by the ivy-clad viaduct which towers above the road. Again the railway opted for a more direct route and in so doing left the loop of the canal almost intact, its line clearly visible heading north-west towards St Julian's Well and Wellow Tunnel.

E WELLOW TUNNEL was the SCC's longest venture into semi-darkness. At 405ft it was over twice as long as Combe Hay; it was also wider (13ft 2in) though, at 7ft, fractionally lower. The tunnel had a towpath which, unlike the rest of the original canal section, was not used as the bed for the 1815 tramway because of the limited headroom on the downward curve of the roof. Instead the canal bed was filled in to accommodate the height of the horse-drawn waggons. Today the tunnel's northern portal is well and truly in the hands of nature, its arch having been walled up; until recently the southern façade lurked unseen – but preserved – behind a farm building but now has a new lease of life, still unseen by most, as a garden feature. Above ground, just before the right-hand turning up by the church, is for the moment as near as the walker is likely to get!

8 Head for the next stile just around the corner at the far end of the field; cross this and continue down diagonally left towards the bed of the canal.

Seepage from St Julian's Well ensures that there is always water in the westerly curve of the canal's northern approach to Wellow Tunnel. The broad horseshoe bend is well defined and both arms can be viewed from the bank above its apex. The bend is not as tight as the one between locks 11 and 10 at Combe Hay, nevertheless two boats meeting here could easily have got themselves into something of a tangle ... mind you, few boats ever used the canal!

9 From the apex of the bend, head up the slope to the large stile in the fence behind; cross this and, keeping close to the right-hand fence, head for a second stile at the top of the field.

From the first stile that last glance back at the canal ditch will have to be the lasting memory of the Radstock line for nowhere else is the bed and line so well preserved, so easily re-created in the mind's eye. As canal and church disappear from view, Wellow itself spreads out into the landscape below.

10 Cross the stile and the one directly opposite and follow the right-hand edge of the next field up the hill and turn left at the top; continue along the top of the field to the gate onto the road and turn right onto it.

11 Walk down towards Upper Twinhoe and turn left at the T-junction; follow the road round two bends and turn right off it and onto the bridle-way just before the third bend.

It's downhill all the way now, down from the ridge that separates the shallow valleys of the Cam and Wellow. Down too to the Dunkerton line of the SCC, to one of the best preserved stretches and one that includes the gateway to the Radstock line, Midford Aqueduct.

12 Veer left at the 'No right of way' sign and follow the lane to the stile on the right, 40 yards beyond the bridge over the Cam, and cross onto the long stretch of canalside path.

F The few surviving remains of the chamber of LOCK 20, the third of the Combe Hay flight, lurk in the undergrowth just east of the stile off Twinhoe Lane. Originally this and its two neighbours to the east were part of the 3-lock flight that obviated the need for a deep cutting further on at the Feeder Cut (see Walk 2), the approach to Jessop's inclined plane; they therefore pre-date the rest of the Combe Hay locks by several years. But, like the rest, they were to the standard narrow-gauge pattern familiar on other canals; 75ft long, 7ft wide, a rise/fall of 6ft regulated by ground paddles, a single top gate and two mitred bottom gates. The chambers of locks 21 and 22 are both easy to find and more intact but have suffered no less than their neighbour at the rampant hands of the encroaching vegetation.

At the apex of the long loop in the canal to the south, a low mound extends out from the embankment into the adjacent field. A recent accidental 'excavation' of the mound revealed fragments of china, glass and clay pipes, the shells of oysters, cockles and mussels and coal and coke ashes which suggests that it might have been a tip set aside for canal boatmen and their families ... a theory given credence by an early OS map that marks the site with two boundary posts.

13 Cross the stile and follow the path round to the right, left under the viaduct and round to the stile just south of the stone bridge.

Though the path passes round the railway viaduct, it is possible to scramble up the viaduct's embankment to look down on the canal as, on the one hand, it sweeps gently south and, on the other, it curves sharply under the stone turnover bridge towards Midford Aqueduct.

G Canal companies sited BOUNDARY POSTS, such as the two either side of the canal just south of the stone bridge, to indicate the limits of their property. As with mileposts these varied in style between one canal and another, those on the SCC being stone and bearing the letters CCC (Coal Canal Company).

H The TURNOVER BRIDGE here started life as a necessity to comply with the legal requirement embodied in all canal Acts that existing highways be maintained. Thus, when the lane between Upper Midford and Twinhoe was bisected by the canal, an appropriate crossing had to be provided. The kind of bridge depended on the volume and type of traffic though generally speaking canal companies honed in on the cheapest option, normally some kind of movable bridge. Between the junction of the canal's two lines and Midford there were, seemingly, towing paths on both sides of the canal – the southern one for traffic using the Radstock arm, the northern one for boats using the Dunkerton line. It was here at Upper Midford that traffic on the latter 'turned over' to and from the northern path.

The roadside house, Hyver Kennels, to the north of the bridge, was originally the *Boatman's Arms* which, needless-to-say, was oft frequented by passing boatmen. Today, canal-side pubs are in; they meet the modern need for comfort and relaxation in an out-of-town setting. For the working boatman they were an integral part of his day-to-day routines and were often built by or on land owned by the canal company. Many were no more than ale-houses that provided relaxation and a good stable, while others were regular meeting places for boatmen and their families. It is not surprising therefore that a pub should have flourished here by the junction of the two arms of the canal . . . even less surprising that both canal and pub have long gone.

14 Continue alongside the canal ditch to another stile, cross this and remain on the clearly defined path, which eventually changes sides, to the main road at Midford.

The public footpath to Midford keeps generally to the south of the canal but between Midford and the entrance to the Radstock arm there was a towing path on both sides, there being no bridge across the entrance. Craft using the Dunkerton line were re-united with the southern towpath via the stone accommodation bridge at Upper Midford.

I The short 3-arched stone span of MIDFORD AQUEDUCT sits astride the Cam Brook at the northern end of the Radstock branch at its junction with the canal's main line. Much of the Bath stone has suffered with time – particularly the western face – but the aqueduct remains a robust testimony to the hopes that once fired those who planned a working waterway between here and Radstock. The eastern face of the main arch (there were two flood arches) still bears an inscribed stone panel, its lettering worn with age:

> MITFORD
> AQUÆDUCT
> ERECTED
> 18   03
> R. TYLER

Beyond the aqueduct there was probably initially only a single channel – the chamber of the one lock that was actually completed – which was used as a transhipment point for the 'temporary' tramroad from Twinhoe. With the construction of a tramway throughout in 1815 this was extended to form a much larger basin, its wharves, sidings and buildings geared to coping with the increase in trade from the Radstock collieries. Thus, from 1815 until the sale of the Radstock Tramway in 1871, Midford Aqueduct and its hinterland of wharves was the only part of the SCC's route to Radstock that was actually in water.

SHOPS: There are none on the walk itself but there is a general stores at the western end of Wellow's main street.

SUSTENANCE: On the walk itself there is the *Hope & Anchor* (Free House) at Midford which offers an excellent selection of food. In Wellow there's the *Fox and Badger* (Ushers), west along the main street.

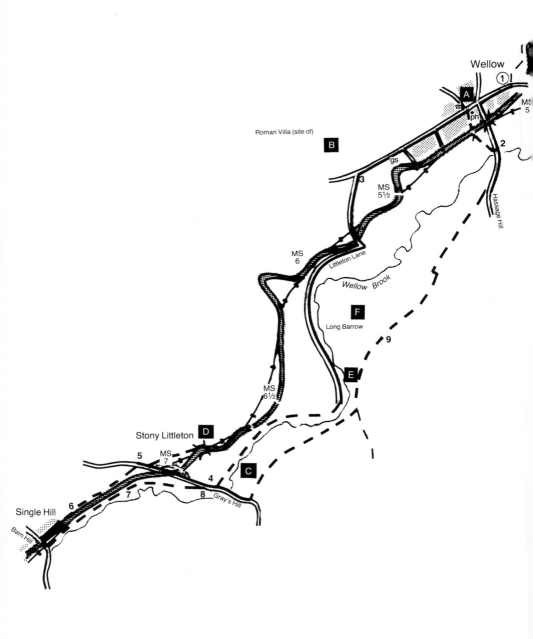

Walk 7 : Wellow to Single Hill.

Start Point: ST 74185834. 6 miles.

Like Walk 3 this is an 'in between' ramble as the Radstock arm makes its quiet way from the complexities of its union with the Dunkerton line towards the Radstock collieries. It is a course that takes it close to outposts of the Wellow valley that were once the haunts of early man, to where even the Rev Skinner found solace.

Access: Main road parking close to Wellow Church should cause no problem though at the western end of the main street there is a signposted car park. Wellow is served by an infrequent (Tues, Wed and Fri) Badgerline service (755/6) between Peasedown St John and Bath; details from Bath (0225) 464446.

In relation to the later track, it is interesting to record that in 1825, Mr William Ashman, of Clandown Colliery, made a locomotive to haul tubs from Radstock to Midford, but the project failed owing to the cast iron rails breaking under its weight; so, here, we have news of the first locomotive in the county, though unfortunately, there is none concerning what became of it.

On Saturdays, the tubs were brushed out and boards placed across them and they were used as passenger vehicles to convey folks from Midford, Wellow and Single Hill to and from Radstock Market.

So here again we find news of the first service in the county, a service that anticipated by about a century the tram services in Bath and Bristol.

(S Lloyd Harvey as quoted in the Somerset Guardian, August 8th 1958)

Stony Littleton Aqueduct

1 Head west from the Church and take the first turning on the left off the main street.

As we have seen (Walk 6), Wellow Tunnel remains an elusive relic of the canal and its heyday. As both its portals survive on private property, its 405ft connecting bore must for the moment remain as an imaginary subterranean channel that is underfoot for only a short time just to the east of the Church.

A Above ground, life goes on in a mellow WELLOW world. The village is a tidy place, an ancient corner of Somerset that looks suspiciously younger than its history would suggest. The church of St Julian goes back to the 14th century; even older is the site of the ford alongside the medieval packhorse bridge over the Wellow Brook. But Mill Lane has seen more recent disturbances in the form of the canal and then the railway. The abutments of the railway viaduct remain, though less discernible is the canal aqueduct that spanned a much narrower lane just to its north. On the western side there is a ramp that probably once led up to a small canal-side wharf where there was a smithy . . . perhaps it was this canal-side blacksmith who was known to have taken home a skull from the Stony Littleton Long Barrow (see below) and used it as a receptacle for nails!

2 Turn right at the ford towards the packhorse bridge, then right again and up the lane that leads uphill from the bridge; turn left onto the main street at the *Fox and Badger*.

The lane back uphill is bisected by the line of the railway (the canal was all but obliterated to facilitate sidings for Wellow Station to the west); its adjacent signal box is a lone and lofty relic of a time not so long ago. The S&DR opened on July 20th 1874, the arrival of the first train here being heralded by a peal of bells from the church tower. Back on the main road there are two further possible south-easterly diversions towards the line of the canal – the first down towards the car park (by the old station), the second down Canteen Lane to where there used to

be a bridge across the cut. Just beyond here the canal swung west towards the road to form a loop while, not surprisingly, the railway took a more direct line south-west. Untouched by the S&DR, some of the canal bed here remains fairly well preserved but, sadly, not accessible.

3 Turn left off the main road and follow Littleton Lane to Greenacres Farm; turn right here onto the narrow metalled track.

B The site of a ROMAN VILLA lies hidden in the pastures due west of the road junction at Wellow. The site has strong connections with Rev Skinner (see Walk 4) who dabbled in such things with more than a little relish and perceived himself as a knowledgeable Antiquarian. His interest in the villa here and particularly its tesselated pavement was clearly an enjoyable diversion from his more mundane duties. He made frequent excursions to the site with friends and other Antiquarians but even here was adept at inducing discord: 'On leaving the place, I was attacked rather unexpectedly by Coles, the farmer, saying I had not satisfied him for the opening of it [the pavement], and had been riding over his wheat; that he thought it was not at all like a gentleman to behave in this manner. In reply I said I had already given what I conceived sufficient satisfaction for every damage to the farmer before I began digging.'

Littleton Lane swings left and then sharp right; the first bend was where the railway crossed, the second where the canal passed beneath at Hiltrow Bridge. The stone wall of the canal embankment, the latter now a cross between a farm-track and a rest home for old vehicles, edges the lane before it is joined once again by the railway, their union sanctified by a large and tightly-packed battery re-charging unit for claustrophobic chickens! Much of the canal's route hereafter has become subservient to the railway or the plough so the walk along Littleton Lane provides a golden opportunity to take in the countryside, contemplate the meaning of life and listen to the chattering of the nearby Wellow Brook. Beyond Greenacres the situation is little changed; there are occasional glimpses of an embankment up on the hillside but this is the line of the railway.

C The observant will not have missed the several war-time PILL-BOXES that punctuate the Wellow valley – see also Walks 6 and 8. It is not widely known that Hitler had designs on this quiet corner of the English countryside . . . the threat was such that pill-boxes and the occasional cluster of tank traps, such as the concrete megaliths on the banks of the Wellow here, were erected as the last line of defence. Der Führer was clearly a clandestine canal enthusiast for similar brick and concrete relics are also a feature of the Kennet & Avon . . . well, it makes more sense than the oft-expressed theory that Britain's canals and river valleys were the basis of its defences!

Just beyond the last pill-box, at right-angles to the track, is Brook Cottage in front of which runs a small stream. Beyond the cottage and its long garden is the railway embankment which spans the stream's valley; out of sight behind this, and parallel to it, is the equivalent canal crossing, Stony Littleton Aqueduct. The stream, of course, is crossed by the track alongside Brook Cottage and shortly afterwards joins Wellow Brook.

4 Turn right up Gray's Hill and right again onto the track just beyond the railway bridge; continue along the right-hand edge of the field to view Stony Littleton Aqueduct before returning to Gray's Hill.

Close to the top of Gray's Hill the line of the canal crosses the road at an angle. Such a 'skew' crossing would have presented the canal's engineers with a difficult bridge-building problem so the road was diverted to the north-east (see map) to facilitate a traditional stone bridge; the road probably recovered its original route after 1815 and the construction of the tramway. Skew bridges, using wedge-shaped blocks of stone, feature on other canals such as the Kennet & Avon but even here the techniques were in their infancy well into the 19th century. The Railway Age benefited from such early experiments and skew bridges and spectacular viaducts soon became commonplace. Similarly the problems associated with gradients, ever a complication for canal engineers, were virtually unknown to

Tank traps on the Wellow Brook at Single Hill

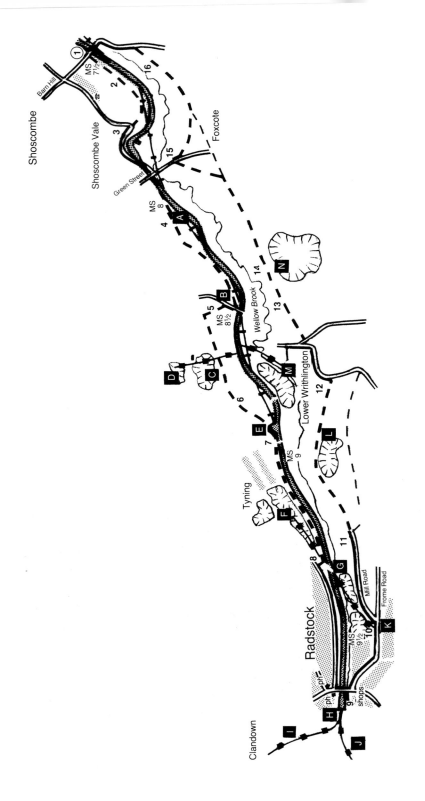

Walk 8 : Single Hill to Radstock.

Start Point: ST 71965620, 6 miles.

The nearer the SCC gets to Radstock the more elusive it becomes. On the other hand the canal's hinterland is studded with the spoils of the local mining industry, ever-present guardians of a way of life not so long gone. This is therefore a walk more about the collieries than the canal . . . but then one would never have existed but for the other.

Access: There is but a single parking space at Single Hill – just north of the eastern abutment of the railway viaduct - and even this involves parking partly on the verge. There is no local bus service though the infrequent (Tues, Wed and Fri) Badgerline service (755/6) between Bath and Peasedown St John does pass along the Wellow Road about ³/₄-mile to the north; details from Bath (0225) 464446.

> At the Quarter sessions for this county, held last week at Wells, Hugh Martin, who commands one of the barges belonging to Mr. H. Guy of Chippenham, was convicted of stealing coals out of his master's barge on the Somerset Coal Canal and selling them to the wife of the lock-keeper at Monkton Combe. The court considering the great mischief and frequency of the offence, as well as the facility of committing it, would have sentenced the prisoner to transportation, and declared their intention of inflicting that punishment on the next offender; but on account of Martin's age, they sentenced him only to three month's imprisonment, and to be whipped severely twice; once on next Thursday, at the inclined plane at Combhay, and the second time on the bridge at Radstock. Phoebe Cockle, the lock-keeper's wife, was found guilty of receiving the stolen goods.
> (Bath Chronicle, January 19th 1804).

Woodborough Basin, two rows of miners' cottages and Tyning Pit's batch

1 Turn west off the road up the track just above and behind the row of cottages; pass through a kissing-gate and cross the field keeping close to the fence on the left.

As with the access road to the properties to the north-east of Single Hill, the road in front of the bungalows and houses going south-west runs atop the line of the canal – and the railway too. There is not a lot to see from the track at the back of the houses, less when the path becomes more hemmed in . . . which is even more frustrating because at this point the line of the canal (just north of the sewage works) remains fairly intact, albeit overgrown, to the south of the railway.

2 Cross the stile in the far left-hand corner of the field and continue along the 'enclosed' path; cross the next stile and follow the path along the top edge of the field and through a kissing-gate to join the road at Shoscombe Vale.

From where the path opens out there are views over to the south-west towards Paglinch Farm. The railway takes a more southerly line while the canal sweeps northwards across it to follow the contour through a gentle horseshoe bend close to the line of the road.

3 Turn left onto the road and follow it to the Green Street 'crossroads'; cross straight across along the track towards Paglinch Farm, leaving this just before the farmyard itself via the stile to the right.

At the apex of the bend a stream was culverted under the tramway (and now goes under the road); this may have originally fed into the canal though it is possible that the local landowner withheld permission to tap it. A little further west there was once a fixed accommodation bridge but the demise of the canal and tramway begat a new road between Single Hill and Green Street and a small hamlet once known as Home House Farm. The road in front of the cottages lies atop the tramway towpath while the paddock to the north is the in-filled canal bed. Green Street

crossed the canal via a draw-bridge which gave access to Foxcote Mill down in the valley below the railway viaduct.

A The track down to PAGLINCH FARM, which predates the canal by over a century and a half, follows the line of the tramway towpath though it is soon joined by the railway from the left. The canal ran along the northern wall of the farm at the western end of which was a stone accommodation bridge that linked the farm's bisected pastures. This went with the coming of the S&DR which provided another crossing about 150 yards due west. The channel from Radstock to the farm was one of the first to be cut as evidenced by the advertisement in the Bath Chronicle *in May 1795 for tenders 'for cutting, embanking, puddling and compleating that part of the canal . . . from Radstock Bridge to Peglinch, . . . for building the several road and occupation bridges.'*

4 Cross two more stiles into another 'enclosed' path and follow this down to the road, Braysdown Lane, via two more stiles; turn right uphill and leave the road to follow the public footpath sign to the left.

B The course of the tramway passed through the small SHOSCOMBE COLLIERY where the lines of the railway and canal part again after a brief encounter. The pit opened in 1828 and closed 30 years later at a time when the SCC could least afford it. It seems to have encroached into the canal bed itself and had a direct connection to the tramway; little remains other than the overgrown and disturbed ground on both sides of the path.

5 Follow the track up to and across the stile and cross the field keeping close to the left-hand edge; cross the stile in the top corner and turn left onto the metalled farm track and continue on straight between the buildings and onto the grass track beyond.

West of Braysdown Lane, which crossed the canal via a stone bridge, much of the canal's line was destroyed by the S&DR for the railway sidings associated with Lower Writhlington Colliery to the south. The path high up on the valley wall looks over Writhlington's bald batch under the western end of which lies the bed of the canal and tramway.

C WOODBOROUGH COLLIERY'S wooded spoil heap is on the right. Not a lot is known about the colliery – which closed around 1840 – but it doesn't appear to have had any direct link with the canal or tramway. The inclined plane from the more northerly Braysdown Colliery was not established until after the closure of Woodborough.

D BRAYSDOWN COLLIERY dates from about 1845 and its inclined tramroad down to the canal tramway from 1885 but the coal was not taken to Midford, rather back along the SCC tramway to Radstock for transhipment via the GWR branch line opened in 1854. The tramroad was subsequently replaced by a new incline down to the S&DR around 1875. The colliery continued working until 1959. Braysdown's batch comes into view on the hillside behind Woodborough's as the path drops back towards the canal at Woodborough Basin.

6 Leave the path via the stile on the left and cross the field diagonally left towards the lone tree and the flat rectangular area at the bottom; leave the field via the stile and continue westwards to cross a redundant stile onto the bed of the railway.

Walking downhill again, the view west is dominated by the spectacular simplicity of two tall terraces of miners' cottages, Lower Whitelands, that nestle in the shadow of two spoil heaps, both of which are associated with Tyning Colliery.

E The purpose of WOODBOROUGH BASIN is unclear as there doesn't appear to have been any colliery tramway link with the canal; Woodborough Colliery is the obvious contender but there is no evidence to support such a theory. The stream culverted under the canal here may

once have been a feeder in which case the basin might have acted as a mini-reservoir similar to the one on the bend south of Bengrove Wood on the Dunkerton line – see Walk 4.

For railway enthusiasts this SCC-side walk is a winner! Between Woodborough Basin and the canal's terminus at Radstock the SCC has been totally obliterated by the railway. But all is not lost, for the cottages at Lower Whitelands and their attendant batches bring some sanity to a landscape that has inevitably become an outpost for a hotch-potch of light industry. Ironically the cottages have few north-facing windows (which would originally have looked out on unlandscaped batches) for, though the southern aspect takes in their impressively long gardens, the view beyond is scarcely pleasing to the eye . . . pity they couldn't be turned round!

F TYNING COLLIERY, which was connected directly to the canal tramway, dates from around 1837 and, having been flooded at least twice, ceased working in 1909. From 1873 the pumping of water from several of the local collieries was centralised here, an operation which continued until 1922. The spoil from both Middle Pit and Ludlow's continued to be tipped here until the 1950s – from the latter via an incline over the tramway. All three were part of the Waldegrave 'empire' (see below) which finally stopped using the SCC tramway to Midford in 1866.

7 Continue west along the bed of the railway and eventually join the parallel path on the right; leave this at the end of the breeze-block wall (by the remains of the kissing-gate) and follow the metalled path to the road beyond the bridge abutments.

G MARBLE ARCH was the name given locally to the 10ft 10in high stone bridge which, from 1857, carried an incline (initially broad-gauge) linking Tyning and Ludlow's Collieries over the SCC tramway and later the S&DR. The limited headroom was a problem to the railway and three small shunting engines were needed to work it when the line of the tramway became in effect a siding. Marble Arch was demolished in 1960 after Ludlow's closed; the brick abutments here are the remains of a small viaduct that carried the same incline over a road.

8 Turn left onto the road alongside the modern houses and follow it into the centre of Radstock.

On one side, new homes . . . on the other miners' cottages. Times have changed and the robust, functional simplicty of the old has given way to the needs of a new, cleaner-cut, generation. Beauty is in the eye of the beholder . . . suffice to say that this particular beholder has strong views on which side of the road he would like to live!

It is perhaps ironic that Radstock, the focal point of Somerset's coalfield, never had a long-term canal link with the wider markets that the SCC bestowed on the collieries around Camerton, Timsbury and Paulton. Although coal had been taken from the earth locally for generations – perhaps even as far back as the Roman occupation – it was not until 1763 that a deep seam (initially 163 yards) was discovered by James Lansdown on land leased from the Waldegrave family. It is not known whether or not

Lansdown had some geological insight although in *The Coal Fields of Gloucestershire and Somerset,* published in 1873, J. Anstie is sceptical: 'The discovery of coal at Radstock must be regarded more as an accident than anything else . . . it is not probable that those who sunk 'Old Pit' at Radstock had any clear notion of the geological structure of the Upper Series basin at that date.' Accident or not, the discovery paved the way for extensive burrowing into the bowels of the earth, and shafts with their attendant buildings and winding wheels soon punctuated the unsuspecting North Somerset landscape. Just opposite the *Waldegrave Arms* at Radstock, a large wheel, part of the winding gear from Kilmersdon Colliery to the south, stands amidst the hustle and bustle of today's traffic, as a lone reminder of a time past.

9 Cross the main road and walk a few yards up the path to the left of the *Waldegrave Arms* before returning to the main road; re-cross this and turn left up the A362 signposted to Frome.

H The RADSTOCK LINE'S TERMINAL BASIN was situated 40 yards below the Waldegrave Arms, so-called after the Waldegrave family

Writhlington Colliery's bald batch

who at one time owned many of the local pits. Nothing remains of the basin nor of the four 70ft docking bays beyond; a walk up the defunct line of the S&DR and a glance north over the iron railings reveals nothing, but is still worth the effort if only to fire the imagination. The basin was probably fed via a leat from the Wellow Brook near where it was crossed by the old Fosse Way about ½-mile to the west. Hereabouts the Wellow is also known as the Somer Stream . . . whatever the name, the local folk-memory recalls that the riparian owners were not keen on its waters being diverted as a canal feeder. Just west of the basin two tramways converged that linked the collieries north-west and west of Radstock to the SCC and subsequently its tramway, though once again there are no visible remains.

I   The ¾-mile CLANDOWN TRAMWAY, opened in 1804, initially served Middle Pit, Old Pit (known originally as Upper Radstock), Smallcombe Colliery and terminated at Clandown Colliery, the deepest pit in the coalfield. It was at Clandown that the colliery's engineer, William Ashman, developed a steam loco-motive (see Walk 7) for use on the tramway; the engine went into service between Clandown and Midford in August 1827, two years before Stevenson's Rocket. Although it could haul nine 27cwt wagons at 3¾ mph on the level, it proved too heavy for the frail track and its use had to be dis-continued. The sale of the SCC tramway to the S&DR in 1871 did not see the immediate demise of the Clandown Tramway; it continued in service into the 1880s when its two remaining collieries, Clandown and Middle, were connected to the railway.

J   The 1½-mile WELTON TRAMWAY also dates from 1804 and initially served only Old Welton Pit though it was extended to the new colliery at Welton Hill. Thus by the time the SCC's tramway opened there were seven collieries with direct connections to Midford; four on the Clandown Tramway, two on the Welton tramway and Ludlow's (see below). In 1834 the newly-opened Wellsway Colliery was also connected to the Welton Tramway. Again the sale of the SCC to the S&DR did not immediately bring about the tramway's closure and coal was still being carried along it until 1880.

10   Continue along the A362 and turn left off it following the sign to Mill Lane Industrial Estate.

K   On the left is the small batch of LUDLOW'S COLLIERY, pronounced locally as 'Ludluss', which opened around 1784 and is therefore one of the coalfield's oldest pits. In 1854 the GWR completed its 8-mile broad gauge branch from Frome to Radstock including a short branch to Ludlow's which soon became, for some pit owners at least, a means of transporting their coal other than on the SCC tramway. This option did not have an immediate effect on the SCC for Lady Waldegrave, who owned Ludlow's and five other pits in the area, made rival owners pay dearly for the privilege of gaining access to the GWR's line. The incline up to Tyning Colliery (see above) was a further extension of the GWR line. In 1897 Wellsway Colliery was connected, with difficulty, to Ludlow's and coal from both collieries was wound up here; for a short time Middle Pit's coal was also brought up here. Ludlow's closed in 1954.

It is perhaps worth putting the coalfields around Radstock into their 'political' context. By 1850 there were three main rival groupings though the pits were often constructed and worked by smaller groups or individuals who did so for their respective landowner. These were the Duchy of Cornwall Collieries (Old Welton, Clandown, and Welton Hill), the Earl Waldegrave's Radstock Collieries (Old Pit, Smallcombe, Middle Pit, Ludlow's, Wellsway and Tyning) and the Writhlington Collieries (Upper Writhlington, Huish, Shoscombe, Lower Writhlington and Braysdown). Not all the collieries within these groupings had any direct connection with the SCC. Similarly Woodborough Colliery doesn't seem to have had any affiliation and in any case closed around 1840, while Foxcote, part of the Writhlington group, was not sunk until 1859.

11 Continue through the industrial estate and carry straight on up the track when the road ends.

There are batches on all sides; those across on the northern side of the valley are given a new perspective and there is a newcomer rising up on the right, the spoils of Upper Writhlington. It is tempting to speculate on what, if anything, this landscape would have to offer without these green hillocks?

L *UPPER WRITHLINGTON COLLIERY began producing coal in 1805, hot on the heels of the opening of the new canal although, like neighbouring Ludlow's, it had no connection to it. Why this should have been so raises the inevitable question about how much it was in fact used before the tramway was built ... something to think about on the walk across the fields from Foxcote to Single Hill. The last coal was brought to the surface here in 1898.*

The ever-green batches of Woodborough and Braysdown dominate the view to the north-east but are themselves soon lost to view by the sombre spoils of Lower Writhlington Colliery. It is perhaps hard to imagine that one day this too will take on a green overcoat ... after, that is, the

NCB landscapes it as it has done recently to Tyning's across the valley.

12 Continue along the track to the T-junction by the church and graveyard and turn left here, following the road to the next junction; cross straight over and follow the path to a barbed-wire gate. Carry on diagonally across to the far left-hand corner of the field and cross onto the raised, 'enclosed' path. Continue over another stile and on through the wooded slopes of the batch.

M *The entrance to LOWER WRITHLINGTON COLLIERY is on the left in the shadow of its spoil heaps. Two shafts were sunk here and opened in 1829 complete with a tramway connection to the SCC. By 1855 its coal was leaving the valley via Radstock rather than Midford and the GWR's broad gauge branch to Frome. This was a costly exercise as access to the railway was over land owned by the Waldegraves and the charge to rival pits was high. Nevertheless, the railway was clearly felt to be a more efficient method of transport and gradually fewer collieries used the SCC. In 1866 the Writhlington Collieries, frustrated by the lack of a direct railway connection to their collieries, began work on the first stage of their own small 2ft 8½in gauge*

Kilmersdon's winding wheel and the *Waldegrave Arms* at Radstock

tramway by linking Lower Writhlington to Foxcote, the line of which is now the 'enclosed' path east from the colliery. Initially coal was transhipped here to the SCC tramway but the Writhlington tramway was extended west and by 1868 had taken in Upper Writhlington, established a coal depot by the Frome Road and linked with the GWR line near Huish Colliery. With the Duchy of Cornwall Collieries only using the SCC tramways as far as the GWR at Radstock, the Waldegrave Collieries not using it at all, the loss of the Writhlington trade was a body blow to the SCC and the demise of its tramway inevitable. The S&DR actually retained the tramway from Welton Hill to Lower Writhlington, though around 1875 reduced the gauge to 3ft 2in and relaid it with wooden sleepers; by 1886 the last remaining length, from Tyning Bridge to Lower Writhlington, was redundant. Lower Writhlington, whose steam winding engine was still in use in 1966, finally closed in 1973, though coal is still extracted from its spoil heap.

13   Where the old tramway clearly turns sharp right up the side of the batch veer left through the woods and down towards the field boundary; negotiate two fences in the bottom left-hand corner after which the woods open out into a field.

N   *The batch on the right belongs to FOXCOTE COLLIERY, pronounced locally as 'Fusscut', which opened in 1859. Foxcote never had any connection with the SCC tramway, coal initially being transported the short distance to Lower Writhlington by road until the Writhlington tramway was built. The pit closed in 1931.*

There are excellent views across the valley towards the canal and railway around Paglinch Farm – the lines of both are clearly visible on the hillside. A little further to the east both lines are again clearly defined across towards Shoscombe Vale, the railway viaduct an obvious landmark.

14   Cross the field keeping to the left-hand edge and go through the gate in the far corner; cross the next field towards the stile and beyond it
cross diagonally left over the next field towards Foxcote Mill and the road.

15 Join the road and turn right and then left off it and over the stile; cross the field diagonally right towards the farm gate; cross this and head towards the stile to the left of the tree stumps-cum-fence posts.

With continuing views across to the canal and railway, and their *raison d'être*, the collieries around Radstock, little more than a memorable surfeit of batches, there is time to reflect on what might have been. A canal was built, of that there is no doubt. But when it opened in 1804 it was an isolated cut with a beginning but no end save the hopes and aspirations of a financially impotent Canal Company and a mile long tramroad. But it did see water – a man was actually drowned in it at Radstock in January 1804 – and at least one known carrier, John Maggs (see Walk 6), tried to earn a living from it. The Canal Company clearly expected it to be used . . . why else was an example made of wretched John Martin at Radstock Bridge? But its incompleteness, as manifested by the tramroad between Twinhoe and Midford, and problems of water supply, which probably explains how John Maggs ran into financial difficulties in a trade ripe for tapping, ensured that it was not to be. Between Midford and Radstock the SCC was destined to be such in name only.

16   Cross the stile and head for another to the left of the house straight ahead, cross this and join the road by the front of the house; turn left onto the road and follow it back to Single Hill.

SHOPS: In Radstock there are shops aplenty.

SUSTENANCE: Shoscombe's *Apple Tree* (Free House) is about half a mile north-west of Single Hill while at Radstock there are two pubs just to the north of the bridge, the *Waldegrave Arms* (Courage) and the *Bell Hotel* (Free House) – both serve food and the former also does accommodation.

The Past in Camera

As with almost all of Britain's canal network, the heyday of the Somersetshire Coal Canal was unrecorded photographically.

The father of photography in Britain, Fox Talbot, lived at Lacock Abbey close to the Wilts & Berks Canal and even if he did ever venture onto its towpath to capture the slow-moving, coal-laden narrow boats (most of which came from the Somersetshire Coal Canal) he would have espied a trade already past its peak.

Photography was still in its infancy at the beginning of the Railway Age; coincidentally the blossoming of both new technologies ran almost parallel which perhaps explains the relative paucity of surviving images of the old order, the people and boats of the inland navigations. The Somersetshire Coal Canal was even more likely to remain unphotographed than its neighbour the Kennet & Avon in that it touched no large cities, such as Bath and Bristol, which, it can be reasonably assumed, spawned more than their fair share of budding photographers.

Thus the archive photographs that follow (all were taken while the canal was working or within 20 years of its closure) do not encompass all of the SCC, merely those parts that some curious eye thought worthy of recording. But words have no such restrictions; the accompanying captions therefore strive to recreate some of the atmosphere and the reality behind the click of a camera, to look beyond the image in time and place.

The photographs are ordered in linear geographic order starting at Dundas Wharf and the Somersetshire Coal Canal's junction with the Kennet & Avon. They do not include any of the Radstock branch and its tramroad. Some photographs may seem to have suffered from the rigours of time, others from lack of imagination on the part of the photographer; such images are included not only to make use of available material but also to punctuate the detailed captions.

1   The autumnal splendour of the Limpley Stoke valley and Conkwell Wood is complemented by the man-made boldness of Dundas Aqueduct and its adjacent basin. The scene is one that belies its industrial and commercial origins, seducing the casual observer into a sense of wonder at its architectural elegance rather than its functional attributes. It was here that the coal-laden narrow boats from the Somerset collieries joined (from the right) the wider waters of the Kennet & Avon en route north and west (to the left) to Bath, or south and east (across the aqueduct) into Wiltshire and beyond. In 1837, at a time when railway competition was still no more than a threat, more than a third of the coal carried, 43,642 tons, passed through the W&B; of this 10,669 tons went the full distance to Abingdon Wharf and the W&B's junction with the Thames. Elegant Dundas Aqueduct may have been, but to the colliers back in the coalfields and the men and boys who worked the boats it was no different to any other part of the canal . . . no more than a means to an end.
c1915, D M McDougall/Kennet & Avon Canal Trust Collection.

74

2 A stone bridge carries the Kennet & Avon's towpath across the entrance to the SCC behind which the stop lock, with a rise/fall of a mere 7 in, holds back its narrower waters. Smoke rises from the lock-keeper's cottage, its occupants overseeing a shallow and weed-choked canal and its redundant lock. It has been accepted, almost without question, that the last coal-laden boat to pass through this lock was Adam Wragg's *Phoebe* in August 1898. This is based on the recollections of Sydney Bourne as published in *Country Life* on May 15th 1951: 'In August, 1898, I travelled with a picnic party in a coal barge from Seend, in Wiltshire, to Dunkerton by way of the Kennet and Avon Canal to its junction with the coal canal at Limpley Stoke . . . the water was only deep enough for the canal boats to carry light loads – that is 12½ tons. Under these circumstances the owner of our boat decided that he could not continue to use the canal, and this was the last journey that was made by our barge from Wragg's Wharf, Seend, to Dunkerton Colliery.' Adam Wragg clearly decided that he had had enough (though he could not have been carrying from Dunkerton Colliery – See Walk 4) but there is no reason to assume that other carriers also ceased trading. The pump at Dunkerton was not shut down until November 11th and it seems unlikely that pumping would have continued for a three month period when no boats were using the canal. In 1898 H A Summers of Bradford-on-Avon was still supplying Somerset coal to the local Gas and Coke Company in his boats *Leopard, Tiger* and *Jack Tar;* similarly Bradford coal merchant, James Randall, had two boats, *Sarah Ann* and *Eliza,* plying the SCC. Perhaps one of these kept Dunkerton Pumping Station in business until the bitter end . . . or perhaps Herbert & Samuel Bird's *The Constant Trader* lived up to its name and was still carrying coal back to Hilperton Wharf.

c1900, D M McDougall/Kennet & Avon Canal Trust Collection.

3 and 4   Canal or no canal, life goes on in and around the lock cottage at Dundas. The cottage and surrounding land (including both sides of the lock) was sold to Joseph Welch and his wife in 1893, the year *before* the canal was put up for sale. Throughout the 1880s the SCCC was in increasing financial difficulties. In 1882 the canal's engineer, William Hill junior, retired and was not replaced; three years later his residence, Caisson House, was sold. Here at Dundas a similar situation arose in the early 1890s and the lock cottage sold off presumably with the dual intention of saving a salary and raising revenue. The derelict and decaying lock, behind which the Welches are posing, did not only see cargoes of coal heading K&A-wards for there was also a trade, albeit small, onto the SCC. Occasionally pit props from Honey Street timber merchants and carriers, Robbins, Lane & Pinnigar, were carried to the collieries, and other K&A traders, such as Bath-based Sydney Hawkins and Gerrish & Co, were known to have worked the canal. In April 1814 the most unusual 'cargo' passed this way . . . a boat-load of Benedictine monks on the last-but-one stage of their journey from Shropshire (where they had sought refuge from the French Revolution) to their new home at Downside by Stratton-on-the-Fosse. Abbot Snow recalls that 'They boarded the boat to the astonishment of the captain, the anchor was duly weighed, the vessel gently glided forward and drifted along after the leisurely steps of the towing horse. The waterway wound round verdant hills, coursed along smiling valleys, through meadow and copse in their fresh spring garb.' The lock-keeper here at Dundas might have been excused a disbelieving smirk as he paid his respects, watched his language and scrutinised all those buckled shoes, long stockings, knee breeches and double-breasted cut-away coats!
c1900 and c1910, Tim Wheeldon Collection.

5   The boatman's first view of Dundas Aqueduct as he slowly rounded the bend under the Bath-Warminster road bridge. But it is a landscape that soon changed as the railway burrowed under the aqueduct's embankment and heralded the end of the short-lived Canal Age. Unlike the K&A, the SCC never witnessed its own age of steam; the few steam-powered craft that worked the K&A in the 1890s were not licensed for the SCC nor is it likely that they could have coped with 'the bad state of the Canal which in its present [1885] condition is disastrous to trade'.
c1900, Tim Wheeldon Collection.

6   A typical SCC stone 'flat-topped' accommodation bridge at Monkton Combe . . . of the kind that unladen K&A barges, heading for Tucking Mill, would have found difficult to negotiate. The horse-drawn narrow boats that passed through this sleepy village were probably an attraction to the boys at the nearby school who will, no doubt, have grown accustomed to the unusual practices of one, Jimmie Mayo. Camerton-born George Tucker recalls that, 'Most of the boats were pulled by horses or mules but there was one man, Jimmie Mayo, who used to pull his own boat. He was a great man and he used to go into the pub and call for a quart of beer at a time, a pint was no good to him.'
c1900. Tim Wheeldon Collection.

7   The view looking west towards Midford and Tucking Mill (off to the right) from William Smith's cottage. In the foreground a team of horses that might well be taking fuller's earth (a natural absorbent clay used as a clarifying agent) from the nearby works of the Fuller's Earth Company. Smith replaced the old Tucking Mill in 1808-9, its foundations probably having become the wharf for the tramroad that came down the hillside from Kingham Stone Quarry at Combe Down. Smith went bankrupt in 1819 which gives further credence to the story that *barges* from the Kennet & Avon worked this far before the lock at Dundas was narrowed to 7ft around 1820. Although most references to boats using the canal refer to 'barges', this term has since come to mean boats *wider* than 7ft, boats capable of navigating the wider locks on the Kennet & Avon. Strictly speaking therefore boats on the SCC were *narrow* boats although in the south-west these were also often known as *long* boats.
c1890, Edward Smith Collection.

8,9 and 10   Three views of the distinctive Weigh-House and toll-office at Midford. It is not clear whether or not the canal was still operating when the second (undated) photo was taken, but it is clearly post-railway (1874). The third photo shows how quickly nature encroaches on the unused and unwanted, how dereliction turns to decay. The first photo speaks for itself, the narrow boat seemingly entering the weighing chamber to have its cargo calculated by being left suspended in

78

a cradle after the water has been drained off. Its horse waits across the cut, being helped by another boatman to resist the temptation of the nearby haystack. Presumably the haystack was intended for the towing horses – there is another in the background to photograph 5. When the Weigh-House was dismantled during the Great War its Bath stone pillars were bought by an antique dealer who, much to his dismay, had to cut them up before carting them away.
c1890, c1898 and c1905, Edward Smith Collection.

14   The Midford to Combe Hay road crosses the entrance to lock 16 of the Combe Hay flight; the lock-keeper's cottage is on the left. This was also a turnover bridge where the towpath changed sides. As well as claiming the lad from Devizes (see Walk 2), two lock-keepers drowned at Combe Hay in 1804 and 1806 . . . and both left the same widow! The unfortunate Frances Heal of Camerton, 'a common prostitute, as she was accustomed to entice the younger colliers and lead them into all manner of mischief', came this way too, in 1815, en route to an untimely death in the Avon. According to Rev Skinner, she accompanied some local bargemen to Bath and was never seen again – the story locally was that one of the men had a grudge against Frances and threw her into the river where her body was later found.
c1905, Gordon Tucker Collection.

15   Lock 1, the top lock of the Combe Hay flight, described by Sydney Bourne thus; 'The top lock was made of iron, no doubt the more easily to hold up the full weight of water, which stretched all the way to Paulton.' The flight itself he recalls as having 'plenty of water in the lower ponds . . . [and] some quite big pike. The lake in the hollow below Southstoke overflowed in a pretty stream and kept the canal at that point well supplied with water; in fact these ponds which were at the lower levels ran over the tops of the locks as the boat went up stage by stage. Above the pond fed by this little stream [presumably at Bull's Nose], however, the water was very low indeed, although the boats going up let down their water behind them and helped a little.'
c1880, Bath Reference Library.

16 Combe Hay's Tunnel with Tunnel House above and behind . . . a peaceful, rural scene that belies the grit and grime of the trade that spawned the canal. A setting altogether inappropriate to the sort of incident that forced Isaac Gingell to publicly apologise for his behaviour on Wednesday, July 7th 1815 in the Combe Hay area: 'Whereas I, Isaac Gingell did on Wednesday last (7th) insult and abuse W Hill, agent to the Somersetshire Coal Canal Company when requested to comply with the regulations of the said Canal by making use of abusive language and speaking contemptuously of the bye-laws, having been guilty of breaking four of them'. Just which four bye-laws Isaac flaunted is not known.
c1880, Bath Reference Library.

17 Once again the intrepid photographer has captured a picture-postcard view . . . this time of Dunkerton's Fosse Way bridge. Perhaps the eye behind the camera has deliberately excluded all signs of activity though, it must be said, that would have been fairly easy to do in 1890, the last year income from tolls exceeded expenditure. The people in the picture might well have contributed to another source of income for the SCCC, the sale of fishing tickets which, in a good year, could amount to as much as £5! *c1890, Bath Reference Library.*

18 This, the smaller of the two aqueducts near Dunkerton, carried the canal over The Hollow and was, if nothing else, functional . . . the Kennet & Avon was the place for the spectacular! Both were completed soon after construction work began and both saw the passage of that first flotilla of five coal-laden boats from Camerton in 1798. The coal was taken by road to Bath by Eleazer Pickwick, the SCCC's Treasurer and a relative of Moses Pickwick who not only ran the *White Hart Inn* at Bath but was also immortalised by Charles Dickens in his *Pickwick Papers.*
c1916, Bath Reference Library.

19 & 20 Dunkerton Pumping Station supplied the canal with its life blood – water. It was also the domain of successive generations of the Bampfylde family who worked on the pumps from 1843. Alfred Bampfylde (photographed here) took over from his father, Charles, in 1885 and was still here when the canal closed in 1898, the year his daughter, Evelyn, was born. Alfred's grandfather, another Charles, was the Rector of Dunkerton but was better known locally as the 'Devil of Dunkerton' – see Walk 3.

After the canal closed, the Bampfyldes lived on in the canal-side cottage, just west of the two pumps, and Evelyn fondly remembers her childhood days here, 'The pumping station was a most pleasant place to live. It was a beautiful walk along the towpath to Combe Hay and father often took us for strolls when we were children. It is a pity it was ever filled in'. Sydney Bourne has an altogether different memory of the area, . . . some distance along the bank towards Dunkerton stood two big pumping engines, of which only one was working. These were designed to raise the water from the Cam Brook to the higher level of the canal . . . a noticeable feature was a large beam of wood which rose up and down, discharging a quantity of water at each stroke; as there was only one of these machines at work, the water was only deep enough for the canal boats to carry light loads – that is 12½ tons.'
c1900, Len Bampfylde Collection.

84

21 Camerton New Pit looking south-east from Red Hill – the colliery workshops are to the left of the pithead gear and New Pit cottages are on the far right. The line of telegraph poles follows the tramroad linking New and Old pits, beyond and parallel to which is the redundant line of the canal. The railway is also out of sight – it ran between the two terraces of cottages. New Pit's batch, the northern slopes of which soon enveloped the canal bed after its closure, is in the left background.
c1905, AIBT Collection.

22   The tramroad down from Lower Conygre Pit to the wharf near Camerton dates from 1859. Such tramroads were a simple and relatively efficient means of transporting coal down to the water's edge; the motive power varied from gravity to men, horses or mules. Accidents did happen. On the SCC's Radstock tramway, for example, someone was killed near Wellow in 1816 by one of the waggons from Welton Colliery near Radstock. The man deemed to have been at fault, William Kelson, paid 10s as compensation.
c1880, Bath Reference Library.

23   The postcard says 'Timsbury' so presumably this idyllic canal scene is somewhere to the west of Radford. Its origins may have been industrial but with or without boats the canal was undoubtedly a pleasant place for a stroll. George Tucker recalls how 'In winter sometimes the boats were frozen in for days. Then they would bring up an iron boat pulled by a team of horses, while on the boat, men rocked it from side to side to break the ice'.
c1900, AIBT Collection.

24 Taken from Lower Engine Pit's batch, the view across Timsbury Basin includes the terminus of the northern tramway, the tramway over the Cam to Upper Engine Pit and all the multifarious buildings that went to make up a busy canal terminal basin. There are boats there too awaiting their cargo of coal before heading back east again. And yet it is by no means a busy scene for already the canal was suffering from the effects of competition from the railways. Be that as it may, such an image is as near as the camera ever got to recording the Somersetshire Coal Canal as a working waterway.
1872, Bath Reference Library.

Appendix A: The Caisson Lock

It is hardly surprising that Robert Weldon's Caisson Lock has generated so much interest, it was, after all, not only a unique contrivance but also one that tried to solve a problem common enough in its day – how to work boats up and down hills efficiently and with minimal water loss. This appendix, therefore, looks at the Caisson Lock from three aspects not already dealt with; comtemporary descriptions of how it actually worked; an artist's impression of what it might have looked like in operation; and reports on its various trials, tribulations and subsequent abandonment.

1 Contemporary Descriptions

William Chapman's *Observations on the various systems of Canal Navigation,* 1797.

> The caisson, or chest is cylindrical; and, in this instance, of sufficient strength to bear the pressure of a column of water 54ft, or upwards; to which it is subjected, when opposite the lower level, on account of the necessity of its being covered when opposed to the entrance of the upper level. It is so balanced that when it has sufficient water within it to float a boat, it is of the same specific gravity as the medium it floats in; and, like an air balloon, it ascends or descends, by a slight increase, or diminution of the relative gravity; which, in this machine, is done by raising out, or admitting an inconsiderable quantity of water. The pit, in which the diving chest moves, has, opposite each level of Canal, a tunnel or opening closed with gates; and is so much higher than the upper Canal as to contain a height of water just sufficient, as already mentioned, to cover the caisson when opposite the upper level. In this, or in its lower position, when run close to, and abutting against, the entrance, it is retained by the water being let out of the short part of the tunnel between the gates of the level, and the end of the caisson. It is then held by the pressure of the column of water intervening between the surface of the pit and that of the Canal to which it is opposed. The gates of the level and Canal are then opened and the boat goes in or out, and, on the gates being again closed, and the water let into the vacancy, the diving chest is ready to proceed to the other level.

John Billingsley's *General View of the Agriculture of the County of Somerset,* 1797.

> As many impediments arise in the progress of Canals; First, from a want of water to supply locks in dry seasons and elevated situations, 2dly. In crossing valleys by expensive aqueducts; 3dly. Tunnelling through hills and high grounds; and 4thly, The great delay occasioned by passing many locks where the unevenness of the country renders it unfavourable for canals;

> R. Weldon, after having devoted many years study and indefatigable labour to avoid these difficulties, and to accomplish this great object, now offers to the publick a description of his Hydrostatick or Caisson Lock.

> The drawing annexed presents a perspective view of the machine or contrivance by which the conveyance is to be effected, and of the inside of the lock, or pound, in which it is immersed.

> A. consists of a trunk or caisson made of wood, and of the dimensions equal to the reception of a commercial vessel of twenty, twenty-five or thirty tons burthen, at each end thereof is a doorway, which the boat, &c is to be floated through into or out of the caisson, and being received therein, and the door then shut, with a given quantity of water

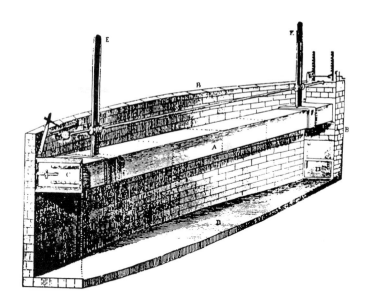

to float the boat, and counterpoise the caisson, so as to make it the same specifick gravity with the water in which it is immersed; it may then be easily raised or lowered at pleasure, either by destroying the equilibrium, by admitting a small quantity of water into the caisson through a valve constructed for that purpose, or by discharging a similar quantity through another valve, or by chains and rollers, as in the drawing annexed, from one level to another, and the boat be floated from the caisson into the canal; the water in the caisson and that in the canal having both the same level whilst the conveyance is effected.

B. Is one side of the bottom, and one end of the lock or cistern in which the caisson is immersed, which is built of free-stone, and of the following dimensions, viz. from the foundations to the top of the wall sixty-six feet, length from out to out eighty-eight feet, width in the middle twenty feet, ditto at each end eleven feet and half, and the perpendicular height from the surface of the lower canal to that of the upper canal forty-six feet.

C. The door at each end of the caisson, which shuts into a rabbet, the frame projecting about three inches beyond the door when shut.

D. The aperture at each end of the cistern or lock, communicating with the upper and lower canal, with a sliding door or gate, which are counterpoised like a common sash, and wound up by wheel and pinion, to receive the end of the caisson, to which it is closely fitted at the time the boat is received or delivered.

R. Weldon having devoted the whole of his time to the superintendence of this great work since the commencement of it, he hopes will be a sufficient excuse for not having the whole history of it ready for the press, but flatters himself to have it complete to lay before the publick (with engravings and references to every part distinct, and carefully copied from the original drawings after which the present machine is constructed) in a few months.

2 The Caisson Lock: an artist's impression of what might have been

Robert Weldon's diagrammatic drawing of his caisson lock (reproduced in part 1 above) is the sole remaining image of this amazing contrivance. What it might have looked like on and in the ground has, since the death of the last eye-witness, been left to the imagination. Mike Chapman, formerly of AIBT, couldn't leave it at that and from all the known facts has tried to put some meat on the bones of Weldon's drawing. The following are Mike's reconstructions, from various aspects, of how the caisson might have worked.

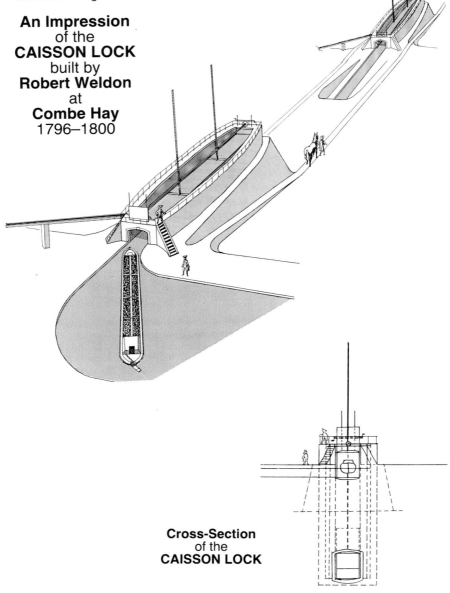

An Impression
of the
CAISSON LOCK
built by
Robert Weldon
at
Combe Hay
1796–1800

Cross-Section
of the
CAISSON LOCK

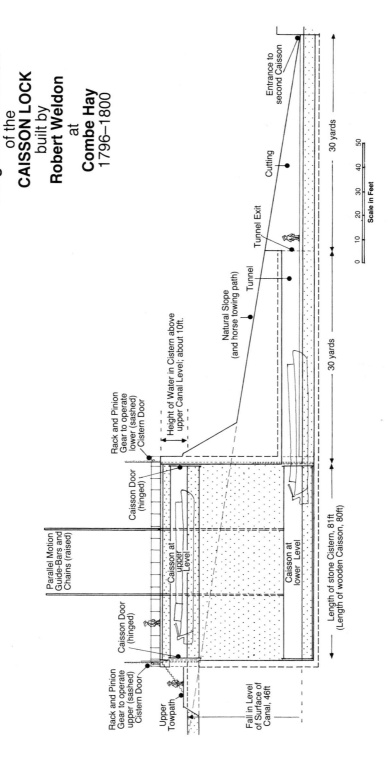

Longitudinal Section
of the
CAISSON LOCK
built by
Robert Weldon
at
Combe Hay
1796–1800

Entrance to second Caisson

30 yards

Cutting

Scale in Feet

0   10   20   30   40   50

Tunnel Exit

Tunnel

Natural Slope
(and horse towing path)

30 yards

Height of Water in Cistern above upper Canal Level; about 10ft.

Rack and Pinion Gear to operate lower (sashed) Cistern Door

Caisson Door (hinged)

Parallel Motion Guide-Bars and Chains (raised)

Caisson at upper Level

Caisson at lower Level

Caisson Door (hinged)

Rack and Pinion Gear to operate upper (sashed) Cistern Door

Upper Towpath

Fall in Level of Surface of Canal, 46ft.

Length of stone Cistern, 81ft
(Length of wooden Caisson, 80ft)

3 The Trials and Tribulations of the Caisson Lock, February 1798—May 1799

Bath Chronicle, February 15th 1798

Friday last, a great company of persons of all ranks were collected at Combhays, to see the Caisson perform its operation of passing the boats from the upper to the lower level. About two o'clock the necessary preparations were made, and the lock nearly filled with water; when, in adjusting a regulating screw of one of the parallel movements, a part of the apparatus gave way, and destroying the parallelism of the caisson, the great body of water it contained, immediately flowing to the lower end, precipitated it, and breaking off the wheels (which kept the whole body parallel and prevented its friction against the sides) threw up the other end within a few feet of the upper door of the lock. Thus for the present was the experiment unfortunately suspended; but as the principle fo the caisson still remains the same, and totally unaffected by this awkward and unforseen circumstance attending the parallel movement, we with confidence look forward to its success in the course of six weeks or two months, when the apparatus will be renewed on a better plan. We have the pleasure to assure the public, that from every investigation that can be made in its present situation, the body of the Caisson itself is not damaged.

Letter from Dudley Clark, Resident Engineer on the Kennet & Avon, to John Rennie, February 1798.

I heard the cassoon was to be tried on Friday last, and went there where a great number of gentlemen and ladies were assembled, the cassoon was then level with the surface of the water, in the chamber and a few feet below the level of the cill of the upper end pond door, they let in some water from the canal (which might have about 2 feet of water) and also from the reservoir. The water some time after it was let in to the chamber became level nearly with that in the canal or upper pond. The cassoon meantime did not rise so much which I expected it would have done, but was 2 or 3 feet under water, but more so to my eye in one end nor the other, that is to say when I observed it, it seemed to me highest at the upper end next the canal. At the same time the water was stopt from the reservoir and I observed to Mr Weldon who was with me, that it was long in coming to a level in the chamber as there was a visible current coming over the cill of the door into the chamber and that it did not fill but rather seemed to me to lower and when they were about adjusting a horizontal rod, in order to adjust the parallel movements. All of a sudden the great joint of cast metal and the large bolt in it, that corrected the parallel motion in the upper end next the canal gave way, by which means the whole of the parallel movement was put into disorder. The end of the cassoon next the tunnel sank to the bottom the other rose and jammed its lower end next the canal upon the building, so that the upper part of the end there, is nearly upon a level with the upper door cill, so that the cassoon lies obliquely in the chamber in the angle of 40 inches perpendicular to 6 feet horizontal or thereabouts. They began to let off the water from the chamber, when I observed to Mr Stevens as certainly wrong, until some plan was fixed upon what was to be done, it was imagined by many that it was broke, but I was not of that opinion, and by sounding at every 6 feet horizontal it was found to be a regular hope.

My opinion is that the cassoon had sprung a leak and by one end being a little lower than the other gave the water within the cassoon an opportunity of getting to that end, and consequently created the weight to make the cassoon descend in the above manner to the great surprise of all present. It will be a great expense and loss of time before it can be tried again if ever. There is about 120 tons of ballast, had the water been all let off it would have strained the whole cassoon and I think by removing the ballast always as they let off the water by degrees will be the safest way.

Bath Chronicle, June 7th 1798

On Monday last, the Caisson-Lock, erected on the Somerset Coal Canal at Combhay, underwent a compleat trial, before the Gentlemen of the Committee, and a numerous assemblage of other persons, when the principles of its action and utility were fully established. The descent of the caisson from the upper to the lower level, the passage of the boat therefrom to the end of the tunnel, its return and admission into the caisson, and its subsequent ascent and discharge at the upper level, may be regarded as a compleat operation; and most unquestionably establish the success of an invention, which, in point of contrivance and utility, may be comtemplated as the greatest discovery of the present age.

After the first experiment, several gentlemen, struck with the facility and safety of the operation, went down in the Caisson to a depth of more than sixty feet, and in like manner returned to the upper level.

In some parts of the machinery, the working was retarded by a few obstructions altogether casual, and which, in future, may be entirely obviated. However, to remove all doubt or anxiety on this occasion Mr. Weldon, the inventor, will undertake to pass through the caisson-lock fifteen hundred tons of goods in twelve hours, with one man to work the machinery, and the assistance of the boatman.

It will ever be recollected with pleasure and gratitude by the public, that the establishment of this most invaluable discovery is to be ascribed to the well-applied patronage and distinguished liberality of the proprietors of the Somerset Coal Canal.

Bath Journal, April 22nd 1799

His Royal Highness [The Prince of Wales] particularly examined every part of the Machinery. He first went into the tunnel, and saw a boat introduced into the body of the Caisson with two or three men in it, when the door of the Caisson was closed, and that part of the Cistern drawn up in its place. In a few minutes after his arrival from the tunnel, the Caisson began to ascend, and in less than two minutes reached the top of the water. His Royal Highness then hastened to the spot opposite the upper door, whence in a few minutes more he had the satisfaction of seeing the boat taken out with the men in it. The doors were again closed and the machine depressed and elevated several times, to show the great command, which the Manager had of it.

His Royal Highness condescended to converse very familiarly with Mr. Weldon on the principles of the Caisson, and to express his entire approbation of it; notwithstanding a continued rain during the whole performance, the Prince's attention was so much engaged in the rapid succession of interesting objects, that he was regardless of the weather, and of the many inconveniences to which the slippery state of the soil exposed him. At his departure he ordered a very handsome present to be given to Mr. Weldon for the benefit of the men who had assisted him in working the Caisson.

Bath Herald, May 4th 1799

On Saturday last, according to our advertisement the preceding day, another trial of the Caisson at Combhay took place. It is impossible to describe the regularity and ease with which this immense body performed its various evolutions. For more than fours hours it was successfully sunk and rais'd again; at one time taking a boat loaded with stones, at another a small boat full of gentlemen and ladies: more than 60 persons descended at different times from the upper to the lower level, and *vice versa*. The time they first went into the boat to that of their coming out did not exceed six minutes and a half. From the number and variety of the experiments then made, the ingenious inventor has discovered many improvements that may be adopted, and simplify the machine to a degree, that in the first trials he thought impossible – a great part of the cumbersome apparatus and consequent expence will be sav'd in future caissons, and the working of them will be rendered as easy as that of the fire engine. It will be most successfully proved, that a single man could work the machine in such a manner as to enable the boatman to introduce his boat into the canal above, and to be ready to prosecute his voyage from the tunnel below in less than seven minutes – such a wonderful control has art given mankind over these powerful agents, air and water! Four or five hundred persons were present on the occasion and testified their unbounded approbation by repeated cheers and plaudits.

Bath Chronicle, May 23rd 1799
The Committee of the Somerset Coal Canal, being desirous of having the present CAISSON CISTERN at Combhay, near Bath, REBUILT, and made Water-tight, (and it being probable that other cisterns of a similar or greater depth may be built on the line of the Canal) invite all Masons competent to such an undertaking, to deliver proposals for erecting and compleating such Work: (sealed) to Mr Weldon at Combhay, on or before the 3rd day of June next.

Plans &c, may be seen at Mr Weldon's; who will shew the ground; and contractors will be required to enter into the security for the Cistern holding water.

The Committee of Management will meet at the York House, Bath, on Tuesday the 4th of June next, at 11 o'clock in the forenoon, for the purpose of considering and determining on proposals that may be delivered.

Bath Chronicle, May 30th 1799
Somerset Coal Canal
The Proprietors of the above Canal are particularly requested to attend the next general meeting on Wednesday 5th of June next, when the following Proposition will be offered for their consideration: –
That CAISSONS, or any other Mode of Conveyance from the Upper to the Lower Level, be suspended until it is ascertained whether the
RAILROAD INCLINED PLANE
(unanimously voted as a temporary expedient at the last Meeting of the Proprietors) be likely to answer the end of a permanent and useful mode of conveyance. Its operation is plain and simple, and the expense of it, compared with the *enormous* one of Caissons, but trifling. The utility of the scheme may be fully known by the next Spring. If any Proprietor should not be able to attend, and approve the above proposition, in preference to the *immediate adoption of Caissons,* he is desired to give his Proxy to a Proprietor's Friend.
May 25th 1799.

The cost in terms of time and money had become, for the SCCC, too much. Any masons' proposals for 'erecting and compleating' the work on the caisson were clearly going to fall on deaf ears. Benjamin Outram's subsequent report on the feasibility of continuing with the caisson was, in financial terms, damning. Robert Weldon was a broken man; his dreams shattered, he left the scene and died in Bristol four years later.

Appendix B

The following article appeared in the April 1983 edition of the national waterways magazine, Canal & Riverboat. *Good Friday that year was April 1st! Omitted from this reprint is the 'doctored' photograph that showed a boat on the canal near Dundas Aqueduct and the telephone number for 'further details' that stopped most people from turning up at Paulton to welcome the boats!*

Somerset Canal Reopening

The Somerset Coal Canal will be reopened on Good Friday. Niall Allsop reports on the work that has gone into this little known restoration project.

Once again Good Friday will herald the beginning of a new boating season. For those forced by lock closures and empty pounds to think in seasonal terms there should be, in theory no hold ups. But for boaters in the south-west there is a special treat in store, the completion of a restoration dream that has continued quietly and purposefully throughout the winter months. On Good Friday the first craft for 85 years will turn right at Dundas Wharf on the Kennet & Avon [the navigable limit of the K&A at the time] onto the Somerset Coal Canal to embark on a historic cruise to Paulton.

A West Country entrepreneur, S.C. Cag, has, almost single-handedly, achieved the impossible. He bought the canal over a two-year period and then systematically 'sold' the amenity value of a viable waterway to the local councils along its route. He offered to finance the complete restoration and asked that there should be local support for the maintenance thereafter. Work began in earnest last Spring with the ingenious replacement of the notorious Combe Hay flight by a single inclined lock powered by horizontal gravity, very much on the continental lines.

Early in March, at the invitation of the Somerset Coal Canal Amenity Group, I visited some of the work sites on the 10½ mile stretch from Dundas to Paulton Basin. It must be said that a lot of work remains to be done, but, if the momentum of what has been achieved so far can be maintained, then Good Friday should indeed be a day to remember.

In restoration terms the canal's route between Dundas and Monkton Combe has always presented a problem as the main line now lies along the goal-line of a hockey pitch at Monkton Combe School! However a study of the original engineer's drawings brought to light an earlier, and still traceable, cut to the north that was abandoned in the late 1790s. Indeed this section is apparently in better shape than some of the original route, which suggests that BWB [British Waterways Board] was unaware of its existence.

The strong stone columns of the Midford weigh-house can never be replaced, though a small plaque marks its site on the bend, just before the short Radstock arm enters from the left. This too is being restored to act as a feeder; water will be pumped up into the original two-arched aqueduct and thence into the canal.

Less than a mile away is Combe Hay where, in the early days, the canal faced one of its major obstacles, a 150ft climb to the coalfields. Experiments with a caisson lock and an inclined plane preceded the inevitable, a flight of 22 locks meandering up the hillside. But no longer, for the Somerset Coal Canal now boasts what must be the eighth wonder of the waterways, the *single inclined lock.* By harnessing the forces of horizontal gravity in an inclined water plane, boats will be raised over 150ft in fifteen minutes! The system, first used successfully on the Swiss canals, has since proved itself on other European waterways.

Above Combe Hay the canal passes under the A367 close to Dunkerton where a new aqueduct nears completion, replacing its high earth neighbour. Between Dunkerton and the erstwhile mining mecca of Camerton, the Somerset Coal Canal faced yet another problem, more diplomatic than structural – Camerton Naturist Club! As luck would have it the canal dissects this peaceful retreat creating in affect *two* camps. A delicate problem that has been sorted out with a fair amount of tongue-in-cheek goodwill on both sides.

A new swing bridge provides access across the cut for club members and two lines of fast-growing conifers are already shooting skywards! 'No Mooring' signs are also being displayed at regular intervals with 'No Lingering' at the bridge – destined to be the only gongoozler-less one in the country!

The last stretch, the two miles to Paulton Basin, has always been in fairly good shape but the wharfside buildings at Paulton are no more. There are plans however for a small museum here, an opportunity for boaters to reflect on the thriving industry that gave this canal its birthright.

Back at Dundas the stop lock, the gateway to the Kennet & Avon, remains unnavigable. But not for long. On Good Friday, if all goes according to plan, that strong stone chamber will see again the passage of boats . . . provided of course they can get onto the Kennet & Avon in the first place!

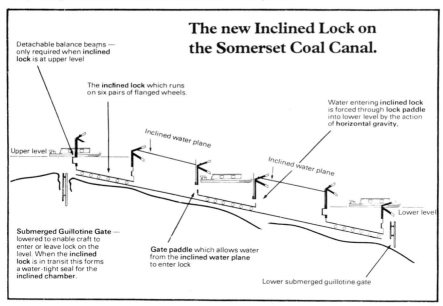

The new Inclined Lock on the Somerset Coal Canal.

Detachable balance beams — only required when **inclined lock** is at upper level

The **inclined lock** which runs on six pairs of flanged wheels.

Water entering **inclined lock** is forced through **lock paddle** into lower level by the action of **horizontal gravity**.

Inclined water plane

Inclined water plane

Upper level

Lower level

Submerged Guillotine Gate — lowered to enable craft to enter or leave lock on the level. When the **inclined lock** is in transit this forms a water-tight seal for the **inclined chamber**.

Gate paddle which allows water from the **inclined water plane** to enter lock

Lower submerged guillotine gate